Business Economics
by Ernest Ludlow Bogart

Address:
HardPress
8345 NW 66TH ST #2561
MIAMI FL 33166-2626
USA
Email: info@hardpress.net

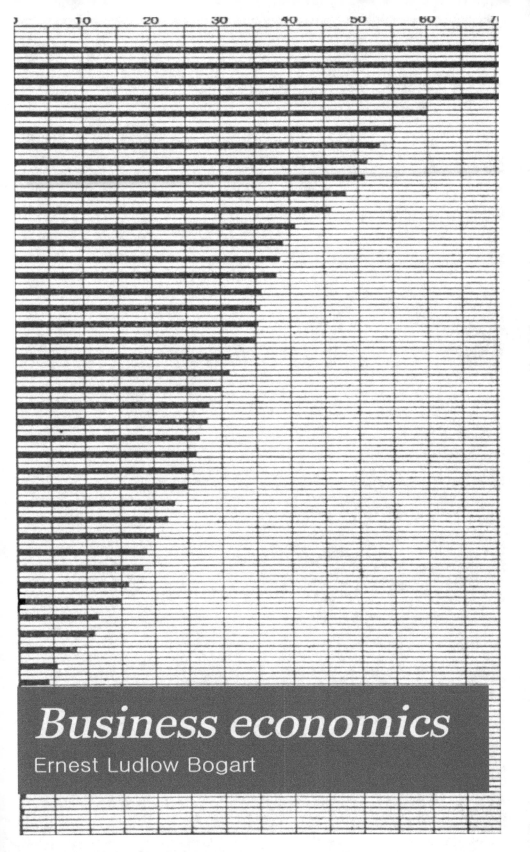

Business economics

Ernest Ludlow Bogart

BUSINESS ADMINISTRATION

The texts listed on this page form the basic material for the LaSalle Business Administration Course and Service. They constitute a library of standard practice in all the important divisions of business management.

Titles	Authors
BUSINESS PSYCHOLOGY .	Hugo Münsterberg, Ph.D., M.D., LL.D. *Harvard University*
PERSONAL EFFICIENCY, APPLIED SALESMANSHIP, AND SALES ADMINISTRATION	Irving R. Allen *Sales Counselor*
BUSINESS LAW I	Samuel D. Hirschl, S.B., J.D. *Member of the Illinois Bar*
BUSINESS LAW II	
BUSINESS ENGLISH . . .	Edwin Herbert Lewis, Ph.D., LL.D. *Lewis Institute, Chicago*
BUSINESS ECONOMICS . .	Ernest Ludlow Bogart, Ph.D. *University of Illinois*
INDUSTRIAL ORGANIZATION AND MANAGEMENT .	Hugo Diemer, M.E. *Pennsylvania State College*
MONEY AND BANKING . .	Henry Parker Willis, Ph.D. *Secretary, Federal Reserve Board*
INVESTMENTS AND SPECULATION	Louis Guenther *Editor, "Financial World"*
ORGANIZING A BUSINESS .	Maurice H. Robinson, Ph.D. *University of Illinois*
FINANCING A BUSINESS . .	Elmer H. Youngman *Editor, "Bankers Magazine"*
ADVERTISING	E. H. Kastor *H. W. Kastor & Sons*
RETAIL MERCHANDISING .	Paul Neystrom, Ph.D. *University of Minnesota*
CREDITS AND COLLECTIONS	Edward M. Skinner *Manager, Wilson Bros.* R. S. White *American Steel & Wire Co.* H. E. Kramer
TRANSPORTATION AND TRAFFIC	I. L. Sharfman, Ph.D. *University of Michigan*
OCEAN TRAFFIC AND TRADE	B. Olney Hough *Editor, "American Exporter"*
ACCOUNTING	Henry Parker Willis, Ph.D.
OFFICE ORGANIZATION AND MANAGEMENT	C. C. Parsons *Manager, Shaw-Walker Co.*

LaSalle Extension University

BUSINESS ECONOMICS

ERNEST L. BOGART, Ph.D.

Professor of Economics, University of Illinois; Author of *Economic
History of the United States, Financial History of Ohio*, etc.

La Salle Extension University
· C h i c a g o · ·
1915

Copyright, 1915
LaSalle Extension University

CONTENTS

BUSINESS ECONOMICS

CHAPTER I

THE MODERN INDUSTRIAL SYSTEM

THE MANORIAL SYSTEM

We shall probably get the clearest idea of the complexity of our modern industrial society if we contrast it briefly with the simpler state of social organization which preceded it. For this purpose we may take the English manor of the eleventh century. At that time England was purely agricultural, and the whole country was divided into manors, of which the lord was regarded as the owner, under feudal conditions, while those who cultivated the land were his tenants. These tenants—villeins and cotters—worked on the lord's land two or three days in the week, and the rest of the time they devoted to the cultivation of their own holdings.

The whole of the land of the manor, both that of the lord and that of the tenants, was cultivated on an elaborate system of joint labor. The land was divided into strips of about half an acre each, and a man's holding might consist of a dozen or more of these strips scattered about in different parts of the manor. This was done in order to secure equality in the fertility and location of each man's land. At that time the prevailing method of agriculture was known as the three-field system, in which one field, comprising about one-third of the manor and

1

containing a portion of the scattered strips of land belonging to the lord and every tenant, was planted with wheat, a second field, comprising another third of the cultivated land, was planted with barley or oats, while the third field was left fallow. The second year saw the second stage of this three-year rotation, one-third of the manor lying fallow each year to recuperate from this exhausting method of cropping; artificial manures were unknown.

Now the significant characteristics of such a manorial society were three. First, it was economically self-sufficient, that is, practically everything that was needed or was consumed on the manor was produced there. There was no need of intercourse with the outside world and there was little contact with it. Salt, iron, and millstones were almost the only commodities that the inhabitants of such a manor had to buy from outsiders. Consequently there was no production of goods for a market, little money, and almost no trade. The few things that were purchased were paid for at prices fixed by custom.

Second, agriculture was carried on under a system of joint labor and under customary methods which did not change from generation to generation. It is clear that as long as all the land of the manor was thrown together for purposes of cultivation into fields on which were planted wheat or barley or which lay fallow, no one individual could cultivate his land differently from his neighbors. Indeed the holdings of the different tenants were not even separated by fences, but only by ridges of grass. On the land which lay fallow the cattle were turned out to graze; if any man had attempted to plant a new crop the third year, his neighbors' cattle would have devoured it under such a system. Production was regulated absolutely by custom, and no opportunity was given for the development of the inventiveness or initiative of the progressive individual.

Third, the tenants were personally unfree, that is, they did not have the liberty of moving freely from place to place, but were bound to the soil which they cultivated. A man could not freely choose either his occupation or his residence. There was no mobility or freedom of movement. Labor was wholly or partly compulsory, and on terms rigidly fixed by custom or by superior authority.

Such a society differs from that of today in almost every point, and offers a startling proof of how far we have progressed in the past eight or nine hundred years. For many of these characteristics, however, we do not need to go back to the English mediaeval manor; the plantation of the South two generations ago, with its system of slave labor, furnishes an illustration more familiar to most of us. With such a condition of industrial development we may now profitably contrast our own of the twentieth century. The chief characteristics of the modern industrial system are the institutions of private property, of competition, and of personal liberty.

PRIVATE PROPERTY

The institution of private property is so familiar to us and so fundamental in modern economic life that we commonly regard it as a natural right. Nevertheless private property, like most other economic institutions, is the result of a long evolution. Primitive man could hardly have had the conception of private property, and when it did begin to emerge, it was at first confined to movables. Indeed we may say that on the mediaeval English manor the private ownership of land did not yet exist in the modern sense. It was found that when each cultivator was permitted to fence in his holding and to call it his own, he cultivated it much more carefully and produced much more. Enclosure led to private property in land and to individual freedom in its use. Today in the United States the possession and transfer of landed property is almost as easy as that of movables.

Private property must be justified on the ground of social utility, because under this method of control so much more is produced than under any system of communal ownership yet tried. But objectors are not wanting who contend that limits should be placed upon this institution and that the right of use, of bequest, and possibly of unlimited acquisition should be brought under social control. The beneficence of private property turns largely upon the existence of competition and individual liberty, and to these we must now turn.

The Nature of Competition

Competition is defined as "the act of seeking or endeavoring to gain what another is endeavoring to gain at the same time." But competition in modern industrial life is not merely a struggle to appropriate an existing good. The very contest, as over the control of a market, may and probably will lead to cheaper and larger production and thus to the benefit of society. Competition is a selective process in our modern economic society, and through it we have the survival of the fittest. "Competition," so runs the proverb, "is the soul of trade." There is, to be sure, a dark side to the picture, for economic competition involves the defeat of the weaker party, but this does not necessarily mean his destruction, for his very failure may sharpen his faculties and secure his ultimate success or at worst he may find employment under his successful rival. But here again it is being urged that competition is brutal and that we should go back to the mediaeval method of regulation by custom or resort to combination and monopoly. We are now witnessing experiments in both directions, but competition still remains the controlling force of modern economic society and bids fair to continue so. It should however be the function of society to raise the ethical level of competition.

INDUSTRIAL LIBERTY

Industrial liberty has been developed even more slowly and painfully than the institution of private property and has in some instances not yet been wholly won. Slavery and serfdom have given way before the higher and more beneficent conception of freedom or liberty. We believe today that a man generally knows what is best for him and will utilize his opportunities to the best advantage; that by giving him a maximum of freedom the welfare of society will at the same time be best promoted. Consequently in our modern industrial society a man is given not only social and religious liberty, but freedom to move, to choose his occupation, to produce and to trade, to associate with his fellows, and to expend his income as he pleases. But here again, while the prevailing rule is liberty, society has found it necessary to lay restrictions upon the abuse of this liberty. It is not enough even to regard the industrial world as a great game in which each may act as he pleases provided only he observes the rules of the game. A higher conception of responsibility and duty must accompany freedom of action if we are to secure the best results.

INDUSTRIAL SOCIETY

The term "industrial society" has already been frequently used and needs a somewhat fuller explanation.

About the year 1760 there took place in England what is usually called the Industrial Revolution. A number of inventions were made which rendered it possible to use steam-driven machinery in the manufacture, first, of textiles and then of other goods. Manufactures were removed from the home, where they had hitherto been carried on, to the factory. Capital began to be used in large masses; machinery displaced hand tools; and the laborer ceased to own the implements with which he worked. Men, machines, and capital were massed in the factory and organized under the management of a new set of industrial organizers for the purpose of producing goods for a world market. The development of such an industrial society has been attended by the minute division of labor, by a growing separation of classes, by concentration of the population in urban centers, by the increasing cost and complexity of machinery, by the development of improved methods of transportation and of credit, by the combination of labor and of capital, by an enormous increase of production, and by the growing concentration of wealth.

CAPITAL IN MODERN INDUSTRY

The introduction of power manufacture completely revolutionized industry. The independent workman with his own tools was superseded by the factory; the small producer has given way in turn to the trust. With the introduction of expensive machinery it became necessary to organize capital on a large scale. Corporations with limited liability were organized for the manufacture of goods, the exploitation of mines, the building of railroads, and the carrying on of trade. As methods of production improved, industry became more and more concentrated, and finally huge trusts took over the operation of combined plants. The business unit has grown increasingly larger, and the need and power of capital have become increasingly important. Capital has played a role of growing significance and has become more and more powerful in modern economic life. Indeed the name ''capitalistic production'' has been applied to modern industry because of the predominant importance of capital in all lines of wealth production.

Impersonal, growing by sheer force of its own momentum, capital is often thought of as intensely selfish and even cruel. Abuses which have arisen in the development of modern capitalistic industry must be remedied, but attacks upon capital itself are misguided and rest upon a mistaken analysis of methods of production.

LABOR IN MODERN INDUSTRY

Before the introduction of the factory system, under the so-called ''domestic'' system of industry, the laborer carried on his work in his own home, where he provided the raw material, owned his own tools, furnished the motive power—his muscles, and was his own master. Today every one of these conditions is changed. The work is carried on in the factory; the raw material, the tools, and the motive power are all provided by the capitalist, the laborer contributing only his own more or less skilled labor, while the conditions under which he carries on his work are largely determined for him. He is no longer his own master. To protect himself against the growing power of capital the worker has organized with his fellows into trade unions. These seek to meet the monopolistic power of capital by exerting a monopolistic control over labor. While they realize that modern productive processes cannot be carried on without capital, they also insist that labor is equally essential. They claim that

capital has received more than its fair share of their joint
production and has exploited labor; consequently they
insist that labor must now demand its just reward and
enforce the claim by strikes and by raising wages.   To
enforce their monopoly, the policy of the closed shop is
often advocated. The interests of capital and labor have
thus often been made to appear antagonistic instead of
complementary to one another.   Frequently in their
struggles the interests of the consumer have been entirely
lost sight of.

THE STATE AND MODERN INDUSTRY

These conflicts in the productive processes of modern
economic society have led many people to look to the state
as the regulator of industry and to invoke state aid or
state intervention along many lines. Maladjustments in
the labor contract, mistaken production, leading perhaps
to speculation and financial panics, abuses of power by
corporate interests, discriminations by railroads, and
similar irregularities are made the excuse for an appeal
to state authority. Some would even go so far as to have
the state take over and manage all productive enterprises; but socialism is as yet a protest rather than a
constructive force.

In the last analysis the state is the regulator of all industrial undertakings, for they all concern society. The
state must hold the balance even and see that fair play
is given to all groups and all classes; but the greatest
amount of freedom compatible with economic justice
must be sought for. It is a difficult question how far the
state must interfere in the conduct or management of
industrial enterprises in order to secure social justice.
There is at present a decided tendency to a strengthening
of the regulative power of the state for the protection of

the weaker classes of society. And yet on the whole the institutions of private property, free competition, and a maximum of individual liberty remain the fundamental conditions of our economic life.

But while under the system of individualism, industrial activities have been multiplied, wealth has been enormously increased, and human progress has been greatly advanced, there still remain many abuses and evils. Many practical economic problems still await solution. Some of these have already been suggested in the preceding paragraphs; others remain to be presented. It is the purpose of this text to apply to some of the more important practical current problems of our modern industrial life the principles of economic science and to endeavor to reach fair and just conclusions on controverted points.

TEST QUESTIONS

1. What were the three distinguishing characteristics of a manorial society?

2. What industrial conditions make impossible the manorial form of industrial organization in our own day?

3. What justification is there for the existence of private property in modern industrial society?

4. How may private property be said to rest upon competition?

5. Does competition tend to perpetuate itself or does it lead inevitably to monopoly?

6. Can personal liberty exist in a state of free competition?

7. Why has the name "capitalistic production" been applied to modern industry?

8. What were the chief characteristics of the domestic system of industry?

9. How does the factory system differ from the domestic system?

10. What is the position of labor in modern industry?

CHAPTER II

THE AGRICULTURAL RESOURCES OF THE UNITED STATES

THE LAND POLICY OF THE UNITED STATES

The land area of the United States, exclusive of Alaska and our island possessions, is a little less than 3,000,000 square miles, or an area somewhat less than the whole of Europe (3,700,000 square miles). Of this about 465,000 square miles, or a little more than one-sixth, still remain in the possession of the federal government and constitute the public domain. The rest, except that which belonged to the original thirteen states, has been given to railways or to the states for educational purposes, or has been sold and given away to individual settlers.

In the disposition of the public domain the policy of the government has, on the whole, been to place it as rapidly as possible in the hands of cultivators and also to use it as a fund to promote internal improvements and education. About 200,000,000 acres had been granted to railroads down to 1871 (at which time land grants were discontinued) to secure their early construction.

This policy has often been bitterly condemned, and it has been contended that the land should have been saved for actual settlers. It may however be said that without such grants the railroads would not have been built at as early a date as they actually were, and that without railroads the land was practically worthless, as it was too far removed from any navigable waterway to have access to

10

a market. Moreover the federal treasury lost nothing, for the sections of land alternating with those granted to the railroads were sold to settlers for $2.50 an acre instead of $1.25, the customary price for the public lands.

The grants of land for educational purposes have been generally approved. Upon such grants rests the establishment of our state agricultural colleges.

The unique and characteristic feature of the land policy of the United States has been the granting of land to the settler upon actual residence and cultivation for five years. Such a grant of 160 acres is called a "homestead" and since 1862 has been made to any citizen who is the head of a family or above the age of twenty-one years. In this way over 230,000,000 acres have been placed without cost in the possession of the actual cultivators. The newer public land states are peopled by proprietors, and there has never grown up in the United States a large class of rich landowners whose land is cultivated by a tenant peasant class, such as exists in England and parts of Europe. For this we must thank not only our land policy, but also the vast extent of unoccupied land that might be had almost for the asking.

Now, however, the public lands available for agriculture have been exhausted; practically all that remains is situated in the arid zone and needs systematic irrigation before it can be made available for any use except that of grazing. There are still many acres of choice land in Indian reservations, and as a consequence of the pressure upon this resource and also because of the improvidence of the old reservation system, the policy has now been adopted of dividing these lands among the Indians in individual ownership, under careful safeguards, and of assimilating the Indians to the rest of the population.

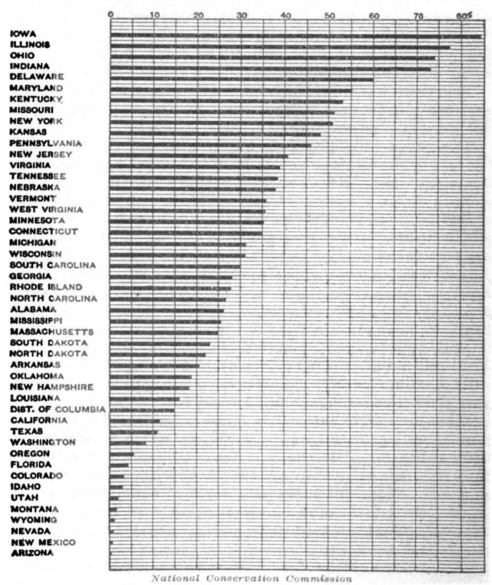

FIG. 1.—Percentage of Improved Land to Total Area

IRRIGATION

The exhaustion of the fertile and well-watered lands of the Mississippi Valley has forced the later comers to have recourse to the arid soils in the almost rainless region west of the one-hundredth meridian of longitude. The character of farming under such climatic conditions must of necessity be very different from what it is in the rainy districts, and the versatility and adaptability of the American farmer are well illustrated by the development which has taken place there. The first effort at the solution of the problem was in irrigation, a method which had been early practised by the Pueblo Indians, and later and most successfully by the Mormon settlers in Utah. By 1910, according to the census, 13,738,657 acres were under irrigation. This represents an increase of 82.7 per cent over the number of acres under irrigation in 1900. The total cost of these irrigation works in 1910 was $307,860,-369.00, or $22.41 for every acre actually watered. The annual cost of operating these great irrigation works was $1.07 per acre.

Up to 1900 most of the construction work had been done by private initiative and the works were completed at comparatively small cost, because the most readily available water was turned upon the most accessible land. Beginning about 1900, very strong pressure was brought to bear upon the federal government to assist in the construction of the larger and more expensive irrigation systems which the situation called for. In response to this demand, Congress, in 1902, provided for the building of irrigation works out of the proceeds from the sales of public lands, and since then some of the largest irrigation systems have been constructed under this policy.

As one sees thousands of acres of land which formerly were a barren waste transformed into some of the most fertile and productive farms in the country, he may easily become eloquent over the wonderful possibilities in irrigation. This enthusiasm has all too often been used by unscrupulous or ignorant promoters in selling land or irrigation bonds, and the losses which have followed have given these securities a bad name with investors. We should bear in mind that there are limits to the irrigation developments of our western states. The water supply is limited and in many sections has already been over-appropriated. There is still room for conservative expansion and for more intensive use of the resources now available, but there are no unlimited opportunities. Experience has shown that regulation and conservation of the limited water supply by government authority are essential to the success of irrigation.

Dry-Farming

A second and even more interesting development of American agriculture is the so-called dry-farming which is being successfully introduced into the semi-arid regions. Carefully selected seeds and plants of crops especially adapted to these climatic conditions are used, and then a very careful and intensive method of tillage is followed. The soil is plowed deep and thoroughly pulverized so that the roots can strike down to the deeper levels and absorb all the moisture available. Extraordinary results have already been attained, and the region that the older geographies labeled ''The Great American Desert'' bids fair to become one of the most flourishing districts of the country.

Size of Farms

That part of the area of the United States which has already been reduced to private ownership is divided into

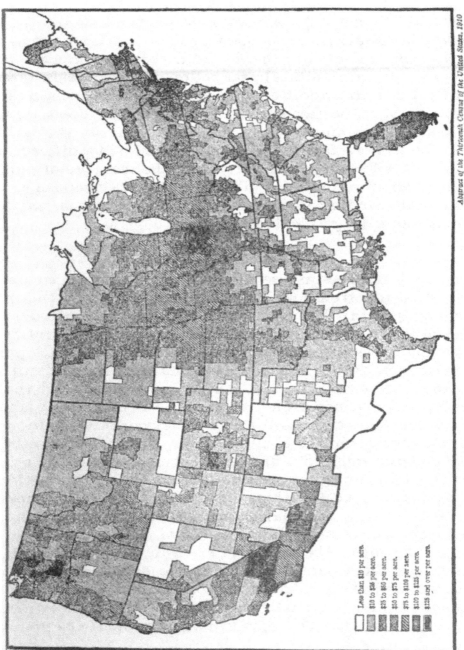

Less than $10 per acre.
$10 to $25 per acre.
$25 to $50 per acre.
$50 to $75 per acre.
$75 to $100 per acre.
$100 to $125 per acre.
$125 and over per acre.

Abstract of the Thirteenth Census of the United States, 1910

6,311,502 farms. As almost half of the land in these
farms is uncultivated, being forest, waste land, or pas-
ture, it is evident that there is still room for a great increase in the agricultural production of the United States
without bringing additional land into the field. The average size of these farms is 138 acres, which looms large
indeed when compared with the 20-acre farms of France
and the 60-acre farms of Great Britain. The difference
is due of course to the difference in the methods of agriculture and the character of the crops, the European conditions demanding intensive cultivation while our methods are still largely extensive.

FARM TENURE

A more important question even than the number and
size of farms, from an economic point of view, is that of
ownership. In 1880, when for the first time the federal
census collected the statistics of farm tenure, the gratify-
ing result was announced that three-quarters (74.5 per
cent) of the farms in the United States were cultivated
by their owners. The last census however showed that
the proportion had fallen to 62.1 per cent in 1910, and
alarm has been expressed that our democratic conditions
of land ownership are giving way to a system of tenantry,
that the ownership of our farms is being concentrated in
fewer hands, and that methods of large-scale production
in agriculture are crushing out the independent farmer
as effectively as they have crowded out the small manufacturer and retailer in other fields. Correctly inter-
preted, however, the statistics seem to indicate that the
growth of the tenant class marks the endeavor of farm
laborers and farmers' sons to establish themselves as independent farmers rather than the fall of former owners
to the rank of tenants. The great majority of the young

men are laborers, the majority of those in middle life are tenants, while the older men are for the most part owners of farms. There seems to be a healthy progress upward in the advancement of wage laborers and farmers' children, first, to tenancy, and finally, with increased ability and capital, to farm ownership. Moreover most of the rented farms are hired by negroes, the change in whose status from slave to tenant marks a great advance.

THE RURAL EXODUS

Another change in our farming population that has been viewed with considerable misgiving is the movement from the farm to the city and the decline in the proportion of the agricultural population to the whole. Indeed the change has been startling, as the United States has passed from a primitive agricultural stage of development to a highly organized manufacturing and commercial stage. From 86.3 per cent of the population in 1820 the percentage of those engaged in agriculture fell steadily until it reached 35.6 per cent in 1910. Many persons have thought that such a movement indicated the desertion of our farms, owing to the greater attraction of the cities and the disappearance of a healthy agricultural population. It has indicated rather a great improvement in the arts of agriculture, whereby one person today, working with improved machinery and better knowledge, can produce nearly three times as much as his grandfather did. The labor set free has gone to the cities—cities of over 8,000 inhabitants now containing two-fifths of our population as compared with one-thirtieth one hundred years ago—and there produces the thousand and one things which contribute to our modern well-being. A smaller number can now raise all the food necessary to feed the population; that the rest are free to do other things must certainly be counted a gain, though the conditions under which work in the factory and life in the city are carried on at present leave much to be desired.

IMPORTANCE OF AGRICULTURE

Writing about 1865, an eminent English traveler, Sir S. Morton Peto, apologized for calling the United States an agricultural country; today he would be spared this worry, for the census of 1910 gave the net value of products of the farm as $5,487,161,000 and of pure manufactures as $8,530,261,000. Indeed since 1890 the value of the manufactures of the country has been larger than of the farm products, and the United States now ranks as one of the leading manufacturing nations of the world. That we are continuing to grow relatively faster as a manufacturing nation is shown by the fact that the total value of our manufacturing products increased 81.2 per cent from 1900 to 1910, while the value of agricultural products increased only 68.6 per cent. Nevertheless the value and amount of the agricultural products are stupendous; the United States leads all countries in the production of dairy products, corn, and wheat, and the greater part of the lumber, meats, tobacco, and cotton which enter into the world's trade come from her forests and fields.

AGRICULTURAL PRODUCTS

While the territory of the United States is well adapted by nature to the cultivation of a great variety of agricultural products, as a matter of fact four main branches furnish the bulk of the value of our total agricultural products. These are the raising of live stock and the production of hay and grain, cotton, and dairy produce. The regional distribution of these products is fairly well marked. Over half of the live stock and of the hay and grain farms are situated in the North Central States; nearly half of the dairy farms are located in the North Atlantic division; practically all the cotton is confined to the southern zone. The same may also be said of tobacco and sugar. The semi-arid region of the West is given over almost exclusively to stock-raising. Illinois and Iowa lead as agricultural states.

EXTENSIVE AND INTENSIVE FARMING

The character of agriculture in the United States, as in all new countries, has hitherto been extensive, that is, a small amount of labor and capital has been applied to a relatively large amount of land, and only the cream of the soil has been skimmed off, as it were. Where labor is dear and land is cheap this is the most economical method for the farmer; and although European critics have severely censured our system of "earth butchery," whereby the fertility of the soil has been exhausted by constant cropping, with no effort to restore the exhausted properties by fertilizing, the practice was justified in colonial days by the conditions which produced it. Now however the practical exhaustion of the free public domain has had the effect of raising the price of lands in the Middle West, and this in turn will cause a more careful and intensive system of cultivation. In other words, as our social and industrial conditions approach more closely those of Europe, we may expect our agricultural methods to do so also. One of the most serious practical problems now confronting the American farmer is the change from the old, wasteful, extensive methods to the new, careful, intensive methods of farming. Those who cannot make the change will complain of the unprofitableness of agriculture, but to those who successfully meet the new conditions the future offers much greater rewards than even the era of free land could produce.

Agriculture as a Science

It has been said that the year 1887 marked the beginning of a new stage of development in American agriculture, namely, that of reorganization, because in that year Congress passed the Experiment Station Act. This caused the application of the principles of experimental science to agriculture on a more comprehensive and systematic scale than had ever been attempted before. Stimulated by the increased activity of the government experiment stations, the agricultural colleges have expanded their work. They are offering practical courses to the farmers, and in co-operation with the railroads some of them are sending out special lecturers, with moving laboratories, to bring the teachings of science as close home to the producers as possible. Finally, the wonderful work being done by Burbank and others in selecting and crossing, by travelers for the federal Agricultural Department in securing from all over the world plants suited to our varied climatic conditions, and by the experiment stations and agricultural colleges in spreading the new knowledge among the farmers and putting it into actual practice—all these departures promise to revolutionize agriculture and to make it, as one writer has said, a learned profession.

Cereals

The production of cereals is the most important branch of agriculture, comprising corn, wheat, oats, barley, rye, buckwheat, and rice. Since the building of the trunk railroads, by which the western territory was given access to a market, the progress of cereal production has been extremely rapid, nor does there seem to be any observable slackening. With the introduction of improved varieties of spring wheat, cereal production is being pushed farther up into Canada and our own Northwest. The center of cereal production has moved steadily westward, from eastern Indiana in 1860 to eastern Iowa in 1910. With the practical exhaustion of unoccupied land suitable for grain-raising in the United States, it is clear that the future extension of the industry depends rather upon improvements in the methods of agriculture than upon the addition of new lands. The very practical problem here presented to the American farmer if he wishes to maintain his supremacy in the world's markets is being nobly and successfully met by the agricultural experiment stations. For example, they are teaching the farmer how to increase his yield of wheat by scientific seed selection and by more careful methods of tillage, from an average of 15.4 bushels per acre for the whole country in 1910 to treble that amount, as is actually produced in France.

Of the separate crops corn is by far the most important, representing 60 per cent of the total value of all cereals produced in 1910. Most of the corn is fed to stock throughout the so-called ''corn belt'' and comes to market in the form of pork and beef. Although corn is very nutritious and is a favorite article of diet in this country in various forms, astonishingly little of it is exported. The development of a foreign market still awaits the enterprise of the American farmer and food manufacturer.

LIVE STOCK

The production of live stock is essentially a frontier industry, and while it will probably always be carried on in the semi-arid grazing districts of the West, which can

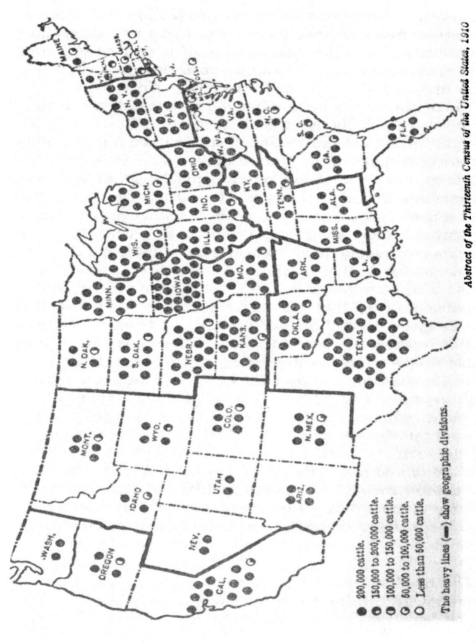

Abstract of the Thirteenth Census of the United States, 1910

Fig. 3.—Cattle on Farms by States, 1910

● 200,000 cattle.
◕ 150,000 to 200,000 cattle.
◑ 100,000 to 150,000 cattle.
◔ 50,000 to 100,000 cattle.
○ Less than 50,000 cattle.

The heavy lines (▬) show geographic divisions.

be reclaimed for agriculture only at considerable expense, it already shows a relative decline. Owing to the great growth of the population, the domestic demand now consumes almost all the meat produced and the exports are declining. This is one of the reasons for the recent rise in the price of meat. The industry is extensive.

Quite the opposite is true of the dairy industry, which is intensive, being carried on for the most part in the vicinity of large cities where land is expensive. The changing character of agriculture and the fact that it is itself a business enterprise which demands a knowledge of market conditions and business methods are well illustrated by the nature of the dairy industry. Dairies are inspected and must conform to certain standards; the milk must be sterilized and shipped, often by special trains, to the cities. Over a third of the butter and practically all of the cheese is now made in factories instead of on the farm; so it is a question whether the latter at least should not be classified as a product of manufacture rather than of agriculture.

COTTON

Of the last of the four important branches of agriculture, namely, cotton-raising, there is not so much to be said. Owing to the intensive nature of its cultivation, machinery has never been applied on a large scale to its production, as was done in the case of hay and grain. The wasteful methods that prevailed in the South before the Civil War have been largely corrected, and the tendency to sterility of the soil has been met by the increased use of fertilizers and scientific rotation of crops. The statistics of cotton crops for the past thirty years do not indicate any decrease in productiveness and show that the point of diminishing returns has not yet been reached.

A peculiar and interesting feature about cotton production is that it is largely in the hands of tenants. The old slave plantations of the South have been broken up into small holdings and many of these are operated by tenants, negroes and whites, who are too poor or too improvident to buy the land outright. The main problems connected with cotton culture are labor problems; and the question has often been anxiously asked whether the free negro will produce as much as the former slave. This can now be confidently answered in the affirmative, although it yet remains to be seen whether he can be made as efficient a producer as his white competitor. Upon the answer to that question depends not merely the future of cotton production, but the economic salvation of the negro himself. The constantly expanding use of cotton goods assures a brilliant future to the cotton-growing states of the South, for not merely is there an assured market in America and Europe, but the primitive peoples of Asia and Africa may be depended upon to absorb increasing quantities of cotton fabrics.

FORESTS

Hand in hand with the heedless extensive methods of agriculture in the past went wasteful use and even destruction of our forest resources. The annual cut of lumber in the United States is today about forty billion feet board measure; at this rate of consumption it is estimated that the present available supply will last only from 35 to 50 years. It will doubtless surprise most readers to learn that about three-fourths of the annual wood cut is consumed as fuel, probably half of our population still depending upon wood instead of coal for fuel. The rapid exhaustion of our forest supplies, with the attendant effects upon moisture, floods, etc., has brought the question of forest preservation to the front as a practical economic problem. We have been squandering the heritage of our children and efforts are now being made to repair some of the loss before we are declared bankrupt. In 1898 the federal government began practical work in the introduction of forestry; this received a great stimulus in 1905 when the care of the national forest reserves, embracing over 60,000,000 acres, was put under the control of the Forest Service. The work has been slowly growing, until in 1915 nearly 4,000 men were employed in the Federal Forest Service. Over 2,000 men are employed for the protective work over the National Forest Reserves and state and private timber lands. This gives about one man for every 80,000 acres as against one for every 1,700 acres in Prussia.

Several states have taken up the movement for the conservation of forests. New York has a forest reserve of nearly 2,000,000 acres, in which it supervises the cutting of timber and attends to reforestation on the cut-over areas. Pennsylvania has a similar reserve of nearly 1,000,000 acres, and other states are following their example. That it is high time to devote attention to the better conservation of this natural resource is made evident by the high and increasing price of lumber, its growing scarcity, and deterioration in quality.

FISHERIES

There is one other natural resource the conditions of whose supply resemble those of forestry and of agriculture in general; this is the fisheries.

As in the case of the other two industries, so with the fisheries, we have been using up our capital and declaring enormous dividends at the expense of the future. The value of the annual catch of fish in the United States, including Alaska, is close to $70,000,000, and is probably exceeded only by the fishing industry of Japan, with Great Britain as a close third. The problem of the better conservation of this resource has been taken in hand by the federal government, through the Fish Commission, and much has been done to repair our early prodigality by restocking lakes and streams with fish. More stringent fish and game laws have also been passed by most of the states, designed to prevent the extermination of the supply.

With careful use, providing for depreciation and restoring the elements destroyed, all of these should prove inexhaustible and should continue to furnish man with food and lumber for all time.

Natural Resources and Economic Laws

After this brief survey of the natural resources of the United States, it is proper to make some practical deductions as to the tendencies of progress in this line. Economists often use the terms "increasing returns" and "diminishing returns." These words explain certain principles which are very applicable to agricultural production.

Law of Increasing Returns

The law of increasing returns simply means that certain industries will yield a proportionately larger increase for any additional time, labor, or thought that may be expended in the productive processes. It is a well-known fact in farming that the extra cost involved in plowing deeper, harrowing finer and at the proper seasons, and selecting the best seed will often give a very much greater relative return. This fact usually accounts for the difference between a thrifty and a poor farmer.

The law of increasing returns gives the scientific farmer his great advantage over the indifferent farmer. It not only compensates for extra work which is applied, but gives something over and above this return, a sort of differential gain. The same land that yields $15 worth of wheat per acre if $5 worth of labor is applied, may yield $25 worth of wheat when $8 worth of labor is applied. In the first case the net yield would be $10 per acre and in the second case it would be $17 per acre. The difference is produced by the operation of the law of increasing returns. The extra $3 applied in labor is paid for and in addition to this sum there is $7 extra for clear profit.

Law of Diminishing Returns

A point is reached, however, in most production when the application of an additional amount of labor will not yield a proportionately large increase. In the example just given, it is likely that if $10 worth of labor were applied to the acre, the yield of wheat would amount to only $26 and the net return would be only $16. The yield would still have been larger than in the former case, but the net return smaller. When such a point is reached, the process responds to the law of diminishing returns. By continuing the process, the returns gradually become less and finally reach a point where further application of labor will bring no additional returns.

Land is peculiarly responsive to these two economic principles. Because it responds to the law of increasing returns, the movement for scientific farming is meeting with such generous response. On the other hand, because all land is subject to the law of diminishing returns, there tends to become a scarcity of land for the people of the globe. If it were not so, the people of New

York or London could be self-supporting upon a single acre of ground by simply applying more and more labor. If such were the case, there could be no problem of over-population. The operation of these two principles must always be borne in mind when the future possibilities of our agricultural resources, or of any other industry subject to the laws of increasing and diminishing returns, are being considered.

TEST QUESTIONS

1. What has been the policy of the United States Government in its disposition of public lands?

2. How has the land policy of the United States assisted the cause of education?

3. Is there any more valuable agricultural land open for entry in the public domain of the United States?

4. How can you account for the strenuous efforts that have been made within recent years for redeeming large sections of arid land by means of irrigation?

5. What is meant by dry-farming?

6. How do the farms of the United States compare in size with those of the European countries? To what is this difference due?

7. What are the main causes for the movement of population from the farm to the city?

8. What four branches of agriculture furnish the bulk of our agricultural products?

9. What condition in the live stock industry is contributing to the high price of meats?

10. Upon what conditions does the future of the cotton crop in the South depend?

11. What is meant by the law of increasing returns in agricultural production? Illustrate.

12. What is meant by the law of diminishing returns?

13. How is scientific farming related to these two natural economic laws?

CHAPTER III

THE MINERAL RESOURCES OF THE UNITED STATES

CHARACTER OF NATURAL RESOURCES

The natural resources of any country may be divided into two broad groups, which call for different treatment and give rise to very different problems. There are, on the one hand, resources which are exhaustible but which can be restored again and, on the other hand, resources which, once exhausted, can never be replaced again by human agency. Under the first head come the soil, the forests, the fisheries, and even the water power, for all of these can be made to yield steady returns to man for thousands of years, if used intelligently. Under the second head belong coal, petroleum, natural gas, and all the minerals; man may discover substitutes or he may economize in the use of these substances, but he can never augment their supply.

In the previous section we considered some of the problems that arise in the use of the soil in agriculture, and those connected with our forests and fisheries. For the most part they had to do with the intelligent use of these agencies and the restoration or repair of the elements destroyed. In this section we are met by a very different problem, namely, the conservation of a limited supply of resources and their most economical application to the needs of mankind.

29

Two Views of Conservation

We can distinguish two contrasting answers to this problem, one careless and optimistic, and the other pessimistic and fearful of the future. According to the former point of view we should not borrow trouble of the future; man's career has been one of constant progress; when he has been confronted with a difficulty he has invariably met it. Indeed necessity has been the most prolific mother of invention. If our coal supplies are exhausted, man will devise means of utilizing the heat of the sun, the force of the tides, the motion of the waves, the stores of electrical energy in the air, all of which will yield inexhaustible supplies of heat and energy. If our stores of iron should fail, some enterprising inventor would surely discover a practicable and commercially profitable method of extracting aluminum from clay. New sources of raw materials will undoubtedly be discovered before the old ones give out, and we may confidently expect that, while the material bases of a high civilization may shift somewhat, they will never crumble and fall.

The other school has sounded a louder note of alarm. At the present rate of consumption the coal and iron deposits of Europe and America must soon be exhausted. The supplies of copper, lead, and other metals in favorable locations are also being consumed at an alarming rate, and no other known supplies are in sight. Within the past century scientific knowledge and engineering skill have combined to unlock the storehouses of the geologic ages, and now like prodigals we are dissipating our fortunes. To treat these exhaustible sources of supply as permanent sources of income, without regard for the future, is based upon unsound theory and must lead to reckless practice.

A Rational Policy of Conservation

As so often in opposing counsels, there is an element of truth in each of these contrasting points of view. However, the safer plan is not to wait until we have exhausted our natural resources before remedying the evil, but to heed the warnings now.

This necessity has been recognized in the activities of our national and state governments and private organizations for conservation. The National Conservation Commission, the Commission on Inland Waterways, and the Commission on Country Life, through the facts which they have collected upon the rate of consumption of the natural resources of the United States and the recommendations which they have made, have turned the eyes of the country to the duty which the present generation owes to the future as a trustee of these riches. Measures have been taken for the better utilization and conservation of these resources through local, state, and national action.

As a result of the national awakening, we may expect to see a more rational use made of the gifts of nature and a better organization of our national life. Heretofore the ideal of our business men has been to exploit, one might almost say pillage, the stores of nature as rapidly as possible; it was a pioneer stage of industry, inevitable but wasteful. From now on the new conception must be the restoration of exhausted elements, where possible, as of the soil and the forests, and the careful use of the non-renewable stores of wealth so that at least we shall not make them engines of destruction, as in the case of floods and devastation occasioned by careless hydraulic mining in the West. Let us now turn to a more detailed consideration of the separate items in our inventory of national wealth.

Coal

Our modern civilization may be said to rest upon coal, for upon its possession depends man's ability to utilize most of the other items of his wealth. Passing over its utility as a fuel to heat our houses, we may observe that without coal it would be impossible to smelt the iron needed in all our industries, to drive the machinery, to run our locomotives or steamboats, or in a word to carry on the manifold activities of our industrial life. According to the United States Geological Survey, there are 335,000 square miles of coal-bearing strata in this country, but the larger part of the coal is too impure to be useful for industrial purposes; it serves in many localities however as domestic fuel, as in the case of the lignite deposits of the Northwest. An estimate by Professor Tarr places the coal-producing area in the United States at not over 50,000 square miles. At the present rate of consumption—over 75,000,000 tons of anthracite and over 375,000,000 tons of bituminous coal in 1913—it has been estimated that the anthracite coal deposits will last for only fifty years longer, while we have only enough bituminous coal for one hundred years.

The large deposits of coal in England and their early development gave that country a great advantage over Europe. But as long ago as 1861 Professor Jevons, a noted English economist, sounded a note of alarm. He prophesied that because of the superior size and character of the coal deposits of America, industrial supremacy must inevitably pass to this country. His prediction has already been verified in the case of coal and iron production and will probably soon prove true of textiles also. The coal deposits of the United States are thirty-seven times as great as those of England, but at the present

rate of mining are threatened with exhaustion at no distant date. It has been estimated that in China there are coal deposits capable of supplying the world with fuel for another thousand years. But such estimates are, in the present state of our knowledge about China, the merest guesses, and, if true, would seem to point to the future industrial supremacy of that country in the world's markets.

Two-thirds of the coal mined in the United States is obtained from the Appalachian field, extending from New York to Alabama, Pennsylvania being the largest coal-producing state in the Union. In the iron and steel industries most of the coal is coked, as it is better for blast-furnace use in this form, giving greater heat and containing less sulphur or other injurious substances than coal. Owing to the smaller bulk and cost of transporting ore, most of the iron and steel industries are situated in the vicinity of the coal supply, as in Pennsylvania, Ohio, Illinois, Alabama, etc.

PETROLEUM

Petroleum, or coal-oil, is closely allied to coal in its origin and distribution and must be classed with it as a most important product, not only for industrial uses, but also because of the contributions it has made to the comforts of living. In its production the United States ranks first, being closely followed by Russia; together these two countries furnish over 90 per cent of the world's supply of petroleum. Enormous economies have been effected in its production and distribution, which latter is done by piping the crude oil underground to the refineries. For illuminating purposes it is the cheapest form of artificial light; as a fuel it is supplanting coal where the latter is dear or its cost of carriage high, as on ocean steamers.

Finally the construction of light and convenient gasoline
motors has given it great importance as a source of motive power.   Natural gas is closely related to petroleum,
but the supply has been so reduced by rapid and reckless
use that it has but a limited economic outlook and is of
local significance only.

Iron

Of all the metals iron must be considered the most
useful for man, far surpassing the so-called precious
metals in economic importance.   Its great utility is so evident that its production and use have often been taken
as a criterion of the material progress of a community.
Iron is the only metal that can be welded and is accordingly of great significance, whether in making strong
machinery, as the shafts of ocean steamships, or the
framework of a twenty-story building, or, in the form of
steel, the most delicate surgical instruments or watch
springs.   Judged by the test of iron ore production, the
United States ranks high, for it turns out about four-
fifths of the world's supply; all of this is used for domestic consumption, in its own blast furnaces, though
much of it is afterwards exported in the form of pig iron
or structural iron or steel.   Though iron is universally
distributed throughout creation, it must occur in large
beds or deposits before it can be profitably mined.

The most favorable situation of an iron ore for profitable
extraction is near good coking coal for smelting and limestone
for a flux, as in the Birmingham district of Alabama; and in
such a situation even low-grade ores can be worked profitably.
Unless this is the case, iron ore cannot be extensively mined
excepting under conditions of great abundance and economical
methods of transportation, as in the Lake Superior district,
where thick and remarkably uniform beds of good ore occur in

such a position that water transportation to the market is possible. Where these conditions do not exist, iron-mining is feasible only on a small scale for the local market. Thus, in the Rocky Mountains there are almost inexhaustible supplies of iron, often of a high grade, which are at present of no value whatsoever.[1]

The most wonderful iron-mining region in the United States and probably in the world lies in the northern part of Michigan and Minnesota, where five ranges or lines of hills contain immense deposits. These lie so near the surface that they can be dug out of open pits at a cost of from 10 to 50 cents a ton, against $1 a ton in a shaft or underground mine. Three-fourths of the iron ore produced in the United States is mined in this district. Its proximity to the lake ports makes possible its transportation to the iron and steel manufacturing centers at very low rates. Machinery has been applied on an immense scale to the work of mining, loading, and unloading the ore. Steam shovels scoop up the ore from the open pit, filling cars at the rate of almost one a minute; the work of loading this into the ore ships at the ports is equally expeditious, only about two hours being required to load an ore ship of 6,000 tons, while the work of unloading is performed for the most part by an endless chain of buckets and traveling cranes.

By these means an ultra-intensive exploitation of these magnificent deposits is taking place and it is a question whether they will not soon be exhausted. "But the Americans," writes Professor Leroy-Beaulieu, a friendly but keen critic of our industrial development, "relying on the constant good-will of nature, are confident that they will discover either new and productive ranges in this district, or rich deposits in other districts."

[1] Tarr, *Economic Geology of the United States*, pp. 7, 119.

PRECIOUS METALS

The precious metals have received more than their fair share of attention, for the industrial progress of the world is much less dependent upon their presence in large and easily obtained quantities than it is upon the more common metals. Nevertheless they are important because of their use in the arts and in exchange as money. In their production the United States stands second, being surpassed in the output of gold by the Transvaal in Africa and in that of silver by Mexico. The production of these metals has always in the world's history proceeded spasmodically, and a speculative spirit has usually been present. More recently, however, scientific geological knowledge and improved metallurgical methods are changing the industry of gold- and silver-mining from a gambling venture to a legitimate industry.

The practical problem at present confronting American gold-mining companies is to reduce expenses, some of the principal bearings having for some years shown signs of exhaustion, as for instance in the Cripple Creek district of Colorado. There is always a chance, however, that new gold fields may be discovered to make good the exhaustion of the old. In the case of silver, on the other hand, the metal is found in such abundance that the present rate of production seems almost indefinitely assured; a slight increase of the price or improvements in the art of extracting the metal will at any time bring enlarged supplies on the market. Africa, Australia, and the United States produce almost all the world's supply of gold, Colorado being the leading state in the last-named country. Mexico and the United States together produce over two-thirds of the world's silver, the leading rank in this country being held by Nevada.

Copper

Among the other metals copper is by far the most important. In primitive civilizations, before the art of smelting iron had been discovered, copper was indispensable because it was so easily malleable; in Homeric times, for instance, armor, utensils, money, etc., were made of copper or alloys of copper (bronze and brass). After an eclipse of some centuries copper has again risen to the front rank by reason of its qualities as a conductor of electricity. The new use of electricity to transmit power and the development of electrical industries have greatly increased the demand for this metal and have caused a great expansion in its production. Here again the United States holds first rank, contributing over half of the world's copper supply. As in the case of iron, the northern peninsula of Michigan is the most important center of copper production, with Montana a close second and Arizona contributing most of the remainder.

Like petroleum, copper production is controlled by a small number of operators, five mining companies alone furnishing one-half of the American supply. Unlike petroleum, it is far from being monopolized, for new and rich supplies lie just on the margin of profitable working and will always be brought into the market whenever the price warrants. One reason for American pre-eminence, aside from the rich stores of the metal, lies in the progress made in the art of refining it by the electrolytic process, considerable foreign ore being brought here to be treated by this method.

Nature has not blessed the United States so abundantly with the minor metals, lead, zinc, and aluminum, while almost all the tin used here has to be imported.

Our Debt to Nature

It is apparent from even this brief and hasty survey of the mineral resources of the United States, comprising those extractive industries which once exhausted can never be restored by man, that this country is wonderfully well supplied with the material means of civilization. Minerals and metals are remarkably abundant and accessible. The wonderful material progress of the United States during the nineteenth century is abundantly explained by this fact, though due credit must also be given to the enterprise, industry, and genius of those who developed these natural resources. The industrial supremacy of the American nation, founded on such a stable material basis, seems well assured. We of this country have been rather inclined to boast of our industrial progress and our material bigness, whereas it must now be apparent that we owe much, if not most, to the bounty of nature. We should therefore see to it, in a proper spirit of humility and thoughtfulness, that we do not waste our heritage, but hand it on as nearly undiminished as possible to our children.

Water Power

There is one other asset in our national wealth which has already contributed much to our progress and is destined to play an even more important role in the future and that is our water power. In colonial days, before the invention of the steam engine and the use of coal, this was of prime importance and determined the location of many a town, inasmuch as the best site was at the "fall line" of the rivers, where water power was obtainable. With the invention of the steam engine and the use of steam as a motive power, industry became less dependent upon water power and moved away from the rivers to the vicinity of coal mines. Now again has come another swing of the pendulum, and with the rise of electricity as a motive power and the harnessing of our streams and waterfalls for the creation of electrical energy, we are beginning to value more highly this source of power. Here again we find the United States wonderfully blessed as compared with other countries. "It is probable," says Shaler, "that, measured in horse power or by manufactured products, the energy derived from the streams of this country is already more valuable than those of all other lands put together." The total amount of direct water power used by manufacturing establishments in 1910 was 1,822,888 horse power, or about 10 per cent of all the power used.

Prior to 1890 the largest use of water power was in its direct application to machinery at the immediate point of development. Since that time, however, the use of electricity as an agency whereby the energy developed by falling water can be transformed and applied to the driving of machinery has entirely changed the conditions under which the power of our streams can be utilized. The practical possibility of transmitting electrical power over long distances—for example, over 200 miles from the Sierras to San Francisco—has removed the necessity of building factories immediately adjacent to water powers, but permits its utilization where most convenient and often where the lack of coal has made the use of steam power impracticable. The best-known example of the development and transmission of electrical energy for industrial purposes is the case of Niagara Falls, but more striking illustrations may be found on the Pacific coast and in the great Keokuk dam across the Mississippi with a capacity of 300,000 horse power. The ex-

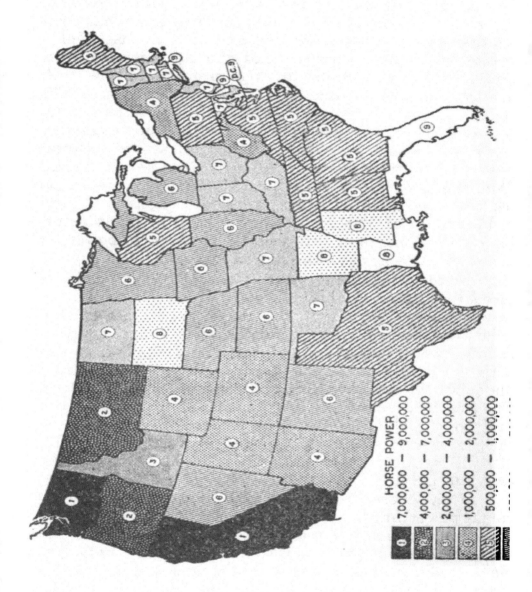

HORSE POWER

7,000,000	— 9,000,000
4,000,000	— 7,000,000
2,000,000	— 4,000,000
1,000,000	— 2,000,000
500,000	— 1,000,000

istence of wonderful opportunities on the Atlantic seaboard gives brilliant promise for the future of manufacturing in this region.

So valuable indeed are these sources of power now seen to be that there is danger that their control may be monopolized by a few shrewd and far-sighted individuals before the general public awakes to a realization of their importance. It has frequently been asserted that there is a "water power trust" already organized for this purpose. The opportunities for wealth-getting have hitherto been so great in this country and the great task of the American people has thus far been so exclusively the one of developing its wonderful natural resources that we have grown careless of our common rights and have permitted private individuals to monopolize a number of limited resources of this character. One of the great practical problems of the future is that of securing the growing value of these natural monopolies to the whole nation, without at the same time retarding the energy and industrial development of the American people.

TEST QUESTIONS

1. Into what groups may the natural resources of our country be divided? Illustrate.

2. What two answers are given to the problem of conserving our natural resources?

3. What are the characteristics of a rational policy of conservation?

4. Where are the leading coal deposits of the country found?

5. At the present rate of use, how long will our known supply of coal last?

6. What is the most favorable situation for iron-ore deposits? State reasons.

7. Where is the most wonderful iron-mining region of the United States located? What makes it such a remarkable region?

8. Why may it be said that the gold- and silver-mining in-dustry is passing from a gambling venture to a legitimate in-dustry?

9. What are the chief gold-producing centers in the United States?

10. Why is copper so very important in modern industry?

11. Upon what factors does activity in the copper-mining re-gions depend?

12. To what extent is water power used in modern industry?

CHAPTER IV

CAPITALISTIC PRODUCTION

Use of Capital in Production

Modern production is usually called "capitalistic" because it involves in its processes the use of a large amount of capital. In a primitive stage of culture man appropriated directly from nature's bounty the food and shelter which he required. But today man has adopted long and round-about methods of producing goods, involving numerous steps between his first efforts and the turning out of the finished articles. He invents tools and machinery to assist him in his work, and while he multiplies the processes of production he also enormously increases the results.

Capital has become absolutely indispensable in modern production and is yearly playing a more important role. At the same time various problems, born of the new conditions, have arisen, such as the growth of large-scale production, the elimination of the small producer and the independent artisan, the growth of trusts, the rhythmic recurrence of speculative periods and industrial crises, the relations of labor and capital, and others similar in character.

The Nature of Capital

What is capital? This question is very pertinent to the topic of capitalistic production. It is easier to describe the main features of a capitalistic society than to explain the nature of capital itself. We may omit the fine distinctions that are made by the economist and describe capital in a few simple words. Capitalistic production is an indirect or a round-about system of production. Labor is first applied to the making of tools and machinery, and these in turn are used for further production. All production is for the ultimate purpose of satisfying human wants. But if, since the beginning of time, men had produced only for immediate consumption, we should still be making our living as the gorilla or chimpanzee. When man first used some of his spare time to chip an axe or an arrow head, he began to create capital. Capital is therefore in the nature of a surplus—something which is taken out of production not for immediate consumption, but to be used in aiding further production.

This explanation of capital makes it clear that it can be increased only by increased savings and by temporary sacrifices. The building of the Panama Canal illustrates this process as clearly in modern industrial life as the illustration of the arrow head in primitive life. The people of the United States have denied themselves the immediate enjoyment of approximately $500,000,000 in order that this great instrument to commerce and industry might be constructed for future use. From this conception of capital, it is evident that it consists only of the concrete instruments made by man. It involves labor and saving. Land and similar elements given by nature are excluded by the definition. If we are to develop our capitalistic system of production, we must produce two classes of wealth: one for immediate consumption to supply the necessities of life and another for future production. Of the three factors in production usually mentioned, namely, land, labor, and capital, man has it in his power to increase the third factor, capital, in proportion as he is willing to save out of present production.

PROGRESS IN CAPITALISTIC PRODUCTION

The most striking phenomenon of the nineteenth century was the great industrial progress of the more developed nations. This is best shown in the following table, taken from Mulhall's *Industries and Wealth of Nations:*

GROWTH OF MANUFACTURES IN THE NINETEENTH CENTURY

COUNTRIES	MILLIONS OF DOLLARS			
	1820	1840	1860	1894
United Kingdom	1,411	1,883	2,808	4,263
France	1,168	1,606	2,092	2,900
Germany	900	1,484	1,995	3,357
Austria	511	852	1,129	1,596
Other states	1,654	2,516	3,455	5,236
Europe	5,644	8,341	11,479	17,352
United States	268	467	1,907	9,498
Total	5,912	8,808	13,386	26,850

Extraordinary as has been this universal growth, the development of manufactures in the United States has been still more marvelous, both absolutely and in relation to other branches of industry. Between 1850 and 1910 both the population and the products of agriculture quadrupled, but the value of manufactured products increased twenty fold and that of capital invested in manufactures thirty fold. The United States, though politically younger than the countries of Europe, is industrially one of the most advanced. The application of labor-saving machinery and of improved and economical methods of production and distribution has probably proceeded further here than in any other land. Nowhere can we study to better advantage, therefore, than in America the problems that have grown out of this advanced capitalism.

CAUSES OF INDUSTRIAL PROGRESS

The causes of this rapid industrial development are enumerated by the census report as five in number: (1) the agricultural resources of the country, (2) the mineral resources, (3) the highly developed transportation facilities, (4) the freedom of trade between states and territories, and (5) the absence of inherited and over-conservative ideas.

We have already considered the wonderful agricultural and mineral resources of the country and have seen how greatly the American people are indebted for their industrial prosperity to the bounty of nature. The magnificent system of inland waterways, comprising over 18,000 miles of navigable rivers, and the railroad system, with over 200,000 miles of track, facilitate a rapid and cheap exchange of products. The enormous domestic market afforded the American manufacturer, larger in consuming capacity than that of any other country in the world, has permitted the economic production of goods on a large scale and a consequent reduction in cost.

Foreigners have often asked the question why, if freedom from tariffs and trade restraints has been a good thing within the United States, freedom of trade with other countries would not prove equally advantageous. In answer to this, James G. Blaine, formerly Secretary of State, wrote: "It is the enjoyment of free trade and protection at the same time which has contributed to the unexampled development and marvelous prosperity of the United States.'' Finally the absence of tradition and of over-conservative ideas handed down from a former and more primitive system of industry has been a great boon. There have been developed traits of energy, inventiveness, and ingenuity, which, aided by a universal system of compulsory free education, have contributed greatly to the material progress of the people.

THE FACTORY SYSTEM

The system under which the production of wealth in a modern industrial nation is carried on is usually called the ''factory system,'' and to this we must now turn, for it is in the factory that the utilization of machinery and capital finds its greatest development. The term is not easily defined, but we may adopt the description given by the late Carroll D. Wright: ''A factory is an establishment where several workmen are collected for the purpose of obtaining greater and cheaper conveniences of labor than they could procure in their own homes, for producing results by their combined efforts which they could not accomplish separately, and for preventing the loss occasioned by carrying articles from place to place during the several necessary processes to complete their manufacture.'' The essential elements in such a system are the minute division of labor, the large use of labor-saving machinery, the increasing specialization and localization of industry, and the concentration of production in fewer and larger establishments with consequent increase of product and reduction of cost.

DIVISION OF LABOR

The division of labor may mean either the separation of occupations or the division of a process into minute parts. An illustration of separation of occupations may be found in the manufacture of a carriage. One factory produces the hubs, another produces the wheels, a third produces the axles, a fourth produces the body, a fifth manufactures the upholstery, a sixth manufactures the hardware, and a seventh (the so-called carriage factory) assembles the parts and places the completed product on the market in the form of a carriage.

As an example of an extreme division of labor, the slaughtering and meat-packing industry offers a classical example, though in this case the use of complex machinery is not involved. Professor Commons [1] writes as follows:

It would be difficult to find another industry where division of labor has been so ingeniously and microscopically worked out. The animal has been surveyed and laid off like a map; and the men have been classified in over thirty specialties and twenty rates of pay, from 16 cents to 50 cents an hour. The 50-cent man is restricted to using the knife on the most delicate parts of the hide (floorman) or to using the ax in splitting the backbone (splitter) and, wherever a less skilled man can be slipped in at 18 cents, 18½ cents, 20 cents, 21 cents, 22½ cents, 24 cents, 25 cents, and so on, a place is made for him, and an occupation mapped out. In working on the hide alone there are nine positions, at eight different rates of pay. A 20-cent man pulls off the tail, a 22½-cent man pounds off another part where the hide separates readily, and the knife of the 40-cent man cuts a different texture and has a different "feel" from that of the 50-cent man. Skill has become specialized to fit the anatomy.

The Classified Index to Occupations, Thirteenth Census of the United States (1910), shows how division of

---

[1] *Quarterly Journal of Economics*, Vol. XIX, p. 3.

labor exists in the cotton mills. It gives the following lines of work:

Manufacturers and proprietors
Officials
Managers and superintendents
Foremen and overseers
Clerks
Apprentices
Back boys
Ballers
Banders
Beaders
Beamers
Bobbin boys
Breaker hands
Card clothiers
Card fixers
Card grinders
Card strippers
Carders
Carpenters
Chainers
Cleaners
Cloth balers
Cloth cutters
Cloth menders
Cloth steamers
Combers
Cotton shakers
Creelers
Designers
Doffers
Doublers
Drawers-in
Drawers and drawing-frame tenders
Dressers
Drillers
Dryers
Dyers
Engineers
Filling carriers
Finishers
Folders
Harness brushers
Harness makers
Helpers
Inspectors
Jack-frame tenders
Laborers
Lappers
Loom fixers
Machinists
Nappers
Oilers
Packers
Pickers
Piecers
Pressmen
Printers
Quillers
Reelers
Ribbers
Roll coverers
Rollers (cloth)
Ropers
Rovers
Roving-frame tenders
Scrubbers
Section hands
Sewers and seamers
Shearers
Sizers
Slasher tenders
Slubber tenders
Sorters
Spare hands
Speeders
Spinners
Spoolers
Spool fixers
Stampers
Starchers
Sweepers
Trimmers
Twisters
Warpers
Washers
Weavers
Winders
Wrappers
Yarn pourers
Other occupations not specified

USE OF MACHINERY

Usually, however, when the division of labor becomes as minute as that described, the routine-like process is handed over to a machine. Indeed Mr. John A. Hobson states as a law of machine industry the fact that as soon as a process becomes perfectly automatic and mechanical a machine is invented which can do the work better and more rapidly than human hands. Hand in hand, therefore, with the subdivision of labor goes the extension of labor-saving machinery. Labor becomes relatively of less importance than capital in the new methods of production, and man becomes a machine tender rather than an independent producer.

There are practical benefits and disadvantages connected with this system. Many writers insist that the effect on the worker is narrowing in the extreme, but Professor Marshall points out that his labor as tender of a machine demands a higher order of intellectual development than that of a handicraftsman, and that he has more leisure, while the product of the present system is immeasurably greater than under the old hand methods. The manufacture of products by machinery has in turn required the making of machines by machinery, as the complex machines of today could not be turned out by hand methods. A characteristic feature of the modern factory system therefore has been the growth of the machine trades, which supply the equipment of the new industry.

LOCALIZATION OF INDUSTRY

With the growing specialization of industry there has gone on an increasing localization in some favored spot or locality. Thus most of the collars and cuffs (85 per cent) manufactured in the United States are made in Troy, N. Y.; 64 per cent of the oyster-canning is carried on in Baltimore; 54 per cent of the gloves are made in Gloversville, N. Y.; 48 per cent of the coke in Connellsville, Pa.; 48 per cent of the brassware in Waterbury, Conn.; and 46 per cent of the carpets in Philadelphia.

While there are undoubted advantages in such localization and specialization in a particular industry, such as reputation, growth of special skill, etc., there are also offsetting disadvantages, such as the complete prostration of the whole community if the particular trade upon which it depends is disastrously affected by trade depression or by a shifting of the industry to some other locality.

Production on a Large Scale

More striking than the concentration of manufactures in particular places has been its concentration in a few large establishments and under the control of fewer individuals. Without entering as yet into the discussion of the trust problem, we may at this time take up the earlier and important tendency of industry to be conducted on a large scale. This concentration into a relatively smaller number of establishments has been going on pretty steadily since 1850 and shows no signs of abatement at this time. In the case of the iron and steel industries, cotton manufactures, and leather goods, the movement is positively startling, an actual decrease in the number of establishments having occurred in the half century. This is most marked in the monopolized industries.

At the same time there has gone on an enormous increase in the size of the individual plant, in the capital employed, the number of men employed, and the value of the product. Almost the only industries which have not yet displayed this tendency are those which are essentially local in their nature, as grist mills, cheese and butter factories, etc. But in general it is characteristic of manufactures in the United States. The same tendency has been manifest in the countries of Europe,

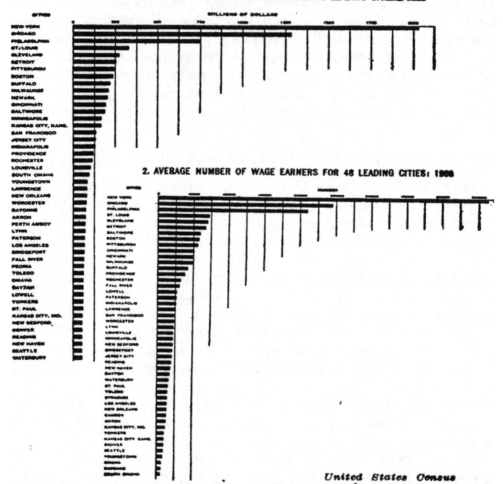

FIG. 7.—Charts Showing the Relative Importance of the Leading American Cities as Manufacturing Centers

though there a system of well-developed and fairly vigorous hand trades has resisted the movement and made the development in this respect much less rapid than in this country.

The following tables explain more in particular the tendency toward concentration since 1850:

	1850	1860	1870	1880	1890	1900	1910	Percentage increase 1910 over 1850
Number of establishments..........	468	542	726	699	699	668	654	40
Average product	$43,600	$97,000	$275,000	$419,000	$683,000	$1,203,500	$2,119,000	4,760
Average capital	$46,700	$82,000	$161,000	$295,000	$591,000	$858,000	$2,282,000	4,787
Average number of employes......	53	65	103	197	250	333	426	704

ALL MANUFACTURES IN THE UNITED STATES

Average per establishment for:	1850	1860	1870	1880	1890	1900	1910	Percentage increase 1910 over 1850
Product	$8,280	$13,420	$13,420	$21,100	$28,070	$25,418	$76,993	830
Capital	$4,330	$7,190	$6,720	$10,960	$19,020	$19,269	$68,638	1,485
Number of employes.......	7.7	9.3	8.1	10.6	13.8	10.4	25	225

ECONOMIES OF LARGE-SCALE PRODUCTION

Large-scale production is more profitable than production on a small scale in all industries which are subject to the law of increasing returns. By this, of course, is meant that the return in product for each additional dollar's worth of labor and capital employed grows greater, the larger the scale on which the enterprise is conducted. When this is true the big enterprise will be able to undersell the little enterprises and eventually to drive them out of business. This is true not only in the competitive industries, but also in those which enjoy a legal or a natural monopoly, as street railways, gas and water plants, etc., all of which show an irresistible tendency to consolidation. Before drawing any conclusions as to the desirability of such a movement, let us examine some of the economies of large-scale production.

The most striking and the most important is the economy in fixed capital. Concentration is a result of machine production. As machinery becomes more expensive, the breaking up of the processes of manufacture into small parts requires more complex and detailed machinery; a larger outlay is requisite for an up-to-date plant. Thus the average amount of capital invested in each iron and steel establishment in the United States increased from $47,000 in 1850 to $2,282,000 in 1910. The head of a steel company in Pittsburgh recently testified before the Industrial Commission that to build and equip a plant for the manufacture of iron and steel under modern conditions would call for an investment of from $20,000,000 to $30,000,000. It is clear that under such conditions of expensive machine methods a small plant would have little chance of existence.

Steam railways afford another good illustration of an industry in which enormous economies are effected by the concentration of a number of small, independent lines under one unified control. Every machine is utilized to the utmost; there is no needless duplication of machinery such as would occur if several small plants divided up the business, while expensive machines to carry on relatively small processes can be profitably installed.

But other economies than those in the use of capital are present in large-scale production. A large concern can hire more expensive and better managers, can afford to experiment with new methods, can effect a more minute and economical division of labor, as for example in the slaughtering business above referred to. A striking economy can also be effected in the utilization of what were formerly waste products, and still are in small concerns. This has been carried furthest in the oil-refining and meat-packing industries; a recent statement of Swift & Company, for instance, alleged that the dividends on the stock were paid out of the by-products, such as neatsfoot oil, land fertilizer, glue, fats, etc. Owing, however, to the generally wasteful methods prevailing in the United States, not so much attention has been given to this point as in England and Germany. A final economy which can be secured by a large business may be mentioned, namely, carrying on allied or subsidiary processes. Thus the Standard Oil Company builds its own pipe lines, makes its own barrels, tin cans, pumps, tanks, sulphuric acid, etc.

WIDENING OF THE MARKET

Such an extension in the size of the single establishment would not of course have been possible if improvements in the arts of communication and transportation had not at the same time immensely widened the market. As long as the market was local and a factory could afford to send its goods over only a limited territory, there was of course a fixed limit to the expansion of that industry. Now, however, when markets are often world-wide and the demand for goods has so enormously increased, when the modern railway and steamship can transport goods cheaply and quickly half around the globe, enterprises can be expanded and conducted on a scale commensurate with the expanded market and improved methods. It is clear then that the tendency to production on a large scale is the logical result of machine methods, that it secures great economies, and that in industries of increasing returns it is absolutely inevitable.

CONCENTRATION IN OTHER INDUSTRIES

But not only in manufacturing is this movement observable. More recently concentration in large establishments has revolutionized the retail trade. Department stores have supplanted the small shops because they can buy on better terms, get cheaper transportation, offer a greater variety to the customer at a lower price, and save him time as well as trouble. The growing ease of communication with central shopping districts, the rapid changes in fashion with the consequent large variety which only a large establishment could afford to carry— all these factors have helped the movement along. There are limits to such a movement, for small tradesmen will always hold the repairing trades and the sale of perishable goods; thus there are no businesses so scattered as the small stores of the butchers and the grocers. But on the whole we may safely conclude that the small storekeeper is doomed now just as the small manufacturer was two or three decades ago. In the carrying trade country carriers and a few cabmen in the cities are the only survivals of the small independent business; the steam railroad and the electric railway have driven the small carrier out of business. In agriculture alone, where concentration is strictly limited by the necessity for intensive cultivation, and in professional and personal service, where the very nature of the business prevents it, there is little or no development in the direction of large-scale methods.

EFFECTS OF INDUSTRIAL CONCENTRATION

The industrial and social effects of this development have been marked in all countries. In the United States the main attention has been given to the organization and development of machinery, and a wonderful industrial advance has followed the movement. The economic readjustments have consequently been made with comparative ease, and the labor set free by the invention of new machines has been reabsorbed in the same or other industries. Consequently the social effects have not been so marked as to call for special emphasis. As the same question presents itself, however, in connection with the more recent trust movement we may profitably defer its discussion to the next section.

STANDARDIZATION

There is one other characteristic feature of modern capitalistic machine industry which deserves special mention, especially as its development has been carried furthest in the United States. Reference is made to the system of stardardization and of interchangeable parts. In no single feature is the contrast between modern machine methods and those of the old hand trades greater. By standardization is meant the production of so-called "standard products" according to some acceptable size, form or shape. In the manufacture of screws or iron beams or even ready-made clothing, for example, certain dimensions and sizes which are best adapted for general use are selected as standard sizes and these are then turned out in large quantities by automatic machinery. The advantages of such a system, in cheapness, quickness of delivery, ability to replace a single broken part, etc., are numerous and manifest.

The possibilities of standardization are strikingly shown in a recent international incident. The Egyptian Government desired a bridge for the Atbara at the earliest possible moment; inquiry was made of the English bridgemakers, but no promise of prompt delivery could be secured. Within twenty-seven days after the tender of the contract was made to an American firm the bridge was ready for shipment. The feat, not a remarkable one, was due to the standardization of bridge material. This in itself was a guarantee of quick delivery and construction.[2]

INTERCHANGEABLE PARTS

Standardization was followed by the system of interchangeable parts, according to which each part of an intricate machine or product is made exactly like the same part in every other machine. The parts can thus be turned out in large quantities and assembled at a single operation. From the standpoint of the consumer or user of the machines thus made, the great merit of the system lies in the fact that he can quickly and at small expense duplicate any broken part. It is today applied to almost every product of large consumption, from agricultural implements and steam engines to watches and nails. By producing machinery on this plan it has been possible for American manufacturers to extend their trade very materially in foreign lands. The newspapers once reported that Mr. E. H. Harriman had expended $65,000,000 in

[2] McVey, *Modern Industrialism*, p. 145.

standardizing the equipment on his railroad systems; while this sum is enormous, it was undoubtedly justified by the increased economy in repairs and operation.

TEST QUESTIONS

1. What is really meant by capital as used in modern industry?

2. How may capital be increased?

3. What five causes does the census report give for the rapid industrial development in the United States?

4. What definition has Carroll D. Wright given of a factory?

5. Illustrate the two meanings which the words "division of labor" may indicate.

6. How does division of labor bring about the introduction of labor-saving machinery?

7. What are some of the economies of large-scale production?

8. What are some of the effects of industrial concentration? Illustrate.

9. How does standardization assist modern production? Give an example of standardization.

CHAPTER V

The Combination Movement

We have already seen how production upon a large scale has superseded production upon a small scale in most important branches of manufactures. We have now to inquire whether production upon a large scale is in turn to be supplanted by single consolidated enterprises, by those combinations of capital known as trusts. Under one of these three conditions industry must be carried on. Few people wish to revert to the stage when production was carried on in small establishments, but warm controversy and difference of opinion still exist as to whether centralized management by a single company or combination offers superior advantages to production by independent competing establishments. The concentration of production in a few large establishments has been followed by the consolidation of these larger units into a single whole.

Since the days of Adam Smith capital has tended to combine for the purpose of fixing prices, and these combinations have passed through several phases. The earliest form is the agreement of independent concerns to fix prices, as was done by the American railroads in their early traffic agreements. The next step was to divide the field, as has been done by the French railways and the American express companies. A third phase of com-

bination was the pool, which attempted to regulate the
output rather than to fix the price or divide the field.
Railway, whisky, beam and other pools were organized
for this purpose, but all broke down because of the difficulty of enforcing the agreement and the temptations to
each member to break it secretly for the sake of the large
profits obtainable. By this time it had become clear that
if a real permanent consolidation of interests was to be
secured by the competing enterprises, some closer form
of combination must be devised which could not be broken
at will by any member. An industrial union and not a
loose confederation must be attained.

Accordingly the next step was taken in 1882 by the
formation of the Standard Oil Trust, so called because
the constituent concerns handed over their business to
the complete control of a central board of trustees, receiving in return trust certificates which entitled them to
dividends. Similar trusts were formed in the whisky,
sugar, and other industries, but were speedily declared
illegal by the federal Supreme Court. By this decision
the form of combination was changed, but the movement
itself was not at all checked.

The next phase and the last was the establishment of
holding corporations, which are organized to buy up and
hold a majority of the stock of a number of individual
corporations, which still retain their corporate existence.
In this way unity of control is secured, to which is added
a certain flexibility; but it is really the trust under another legal form. Where pooling and combination by
means of holding companies have been forbidden by law,
as in the case of railroad companies, actual consolidation
has often taken place, though when trusts are spoken of
the other form of combination is more often meant. From
the point of view of business organization the holding

company is simply an extension of the principle of the corporation, and to a consideration of this we must therefore turn.

INDIVIDUAL AND PARTNERSHIP ORGANIZATION

There are three classes of establishments by which industry is carried on—those which are the property of an individual, those which belong to partnerships or firms of unlimited liability, and those which belong to corporations of limited liability. The usefulness of the individual system is of course limited to small undertakings, where but little capital and credit are necessary; this form of organization still dominates the field in agriculture, in the small retail trade, and in the repairing industries. The partnership is a joint undertaking by two or more individuals and makes larger enterprises possible, but as each individual is liable for all obligations of the firm or his partners his personal liability is greatly increased. It is well adapted to certain undertakings, such as moderate-sized mercantile establishments and professional firms, owing to a certain elasticity in the contractual relations of its members, but it is not suited to large industrial ventures, both because of the excessive personal liability and because of the necessity of dissolving the partnership upon the death, withdrawal, or insolvency of any member.

CORPORATIONS

The advantage of the corporation lies in the fact that it has a continuous existence, and that the liability of the shareholders is limited to the amount of capital actually contributed by each; it is well adapted to modern enterprise because it permits the summation of large amounts of capital from a number of small savers and centralizes

the use of this capital in the most economical manner.
There may thus be concentration of management without
concentration of ownership. The federal census report
on manufactures in 1910 showed that, although only one-
fourth of the manufacturing establishments were organized as corporations, yet they produced 79 per cent of
the total manufactures in money value. The relative
number of corporate enterprises showed an increase of
nearly 100 per cent over that of 1900. In the field of
transportation, corporations are in almost exclusive
control. Most banks and insurance companies are organized under this form, while mercantile and industrial
undertakings are being more and more generally organized as corporations. Not merely are most of our business enterprises being conducted under corporate form
and organization, but most recently, as has been already
pointed out, there has been a movement to combine individual corporations into larger concerns, or trusts. The
trust is usually thought of as a monopoly and, while not
necessarily so, it usually does exercise monopoly control;
but for the present we shall consider the trust problem
from the standpoint of business organization, deferring
to the end of the section the discussion of monopoly.

TRUSTS

The trust movement may be said to have begun with
the formation of the Standard Oil Trust in 1882, but
down to 1898 its progress was slow. Beginning with the
revival of prosperity in 1898, however, there ensued a
veritable stampede of business managers to enter into
combinations. During the next three years 149 large
combinations, with a capital of over $3,000,000,000, were
formed. The movement spent most of its force by 1902,
though it is by no means at an end yet. A few figures

from reliable authorities will make clear the extent of the movement. According to the New York Journal of Commerce, industrial (that is, manufacturing and commercial) and gas trusts were organized in the United States between 1860 and 1900, not including combinations in banking, shipping, railroads, etc., as shown in the accompanying table:

DECADE	NUMBER ORGANIZED	TOTAL NOMINAL CAPITAL
1860-69	2	$ 13,000,000
1870-79	4	135,000,000
1880-89	18	288,000,000
1890-99	157	3,150,000,000
Total, 40 years	181	$3,586,000,000

Another more recent list by John Moody [1] gives the number of industrial trusts organized down to January 1, 1904, as 318; these have acquired or control 5,288 plants and have a total nominal capital of $7,246,342,533. A movement so general and widespread and of such gigantic proportions must have had some powerful and intelligible causes behind it. For it was not confined to the United States, but was equally observable in such industrially diverse countries as England, France, Germany, Russia, and other European nations.

CAUSES OF THE TRUST MOVEMENT

The most important and general cause was the desire to secure the legitimate economies of large-scale production. A combined or federated industry may secure even

[1] *The Truth About the Trusts*, p. 469.

greater economies than a single large factory. These have been concisely stated as follows: [2]

The cost of management, amount of stock carried, advertising, cost of selling the product, may all be smaller per unit of product. A large aggregation can control credit better and escape loss from bad debts. By regulating and equalizing the output in the different localities, it can run more nearly full time. Being acquainted with the entire situation it can reduce the friction. A strong combination has advantages in shipment. It can have a clearing-house for orders and ship from the nearest source of supply. The least efficient factories can be first closed when demand falls off. Factories can be specialized to produce that for which each is best fitted. The magnitude of the industry and its presence in different localities strengthens its influence with the railroads. Its political as well as its economic power is increased.

ECONOMIES IN MARKETING

Many of these economies of production are not new to these trusts, but have been secured equally by large-scale manufacturing establishments. Some of the savings, especially in buying raw material and marketing their products, are peculiar to the trusts and mark a more efficient mode of organization than mere concentration of industry in single large establishments. Thus it has been found possible to dispense with a great number of traveling salesmen, of whom it was said that 30,000 lost their positions in the year 1898 alone. When the whisky trust was formed only twelve of the eighty distilleries entering into the combination were kept running, but as these were the largest, best located, and best equipped, and were run at their full capacity, they were able to turn out as much as all had done before and at an immense

---

[2] Fetter, *Principles of Economics*, p. 321.

economy. The saving of cross freights by having an order filled from the plant most conveniently located is considerable; Mr. Gates estimated the saving of the American Steel & Wire Company in this single point at $500,000 a year. Such an economy could not be secured by a single establishment, no matter how well organized or on how large a scale.

ECONOMIES IN INTEGRATION

The specialization of particular factories to do special processes is well illustrated by the organization of the United States Steel Corporation. The growth of this combination is an example not only of consolidation, but of the integration of industry, that is, the grouping together under one control of a whole series of industries, including the economical use of by-products. From the mining of the ore and coal, through the processes of carrying it to the furnaces, coking the coal and making the pig iron, manufacturing the latter into the finished forms of iron and steel products, and down to the marketing of the latter, every step is carried on under the control of the United States Steel Corporation. The assets of the company were stated as follows soon after its organization, and they illustrate the magnitude and scope of its operations:

Iron and Bessemer ore properties	$ 700,000,000
Plants, mills, machinery, etc.	300,000,000
Coal and coke fields	100,000,000
Railroads, ships, etc.	80,000,000
Blast furnaces	48,000,000
Natural gas fields	20,000,000
Limestone properties	4,000,000
Cash and cash assets	148,251,000
Total	$1,400,251,000

THE INFLUENCE OF PROMOTERS

In addition to economies due to improvements in methods of organization, production, and marketing, another cause for the sudden and vigorous outburst of trust promotion in the years 1898-1902 may be found in the profits to be secured by promoters and organizers. After the successful launching of the first few trusts, with their undoubted economies and advantages, the movement was taken in hand by professional promoters, who organized combinations, often with the help of underwriters, in every branch of industry where there was any promise of profit. That many of these were artificial or premature is evident from the financial results. Of the 183 industrial combinations enumerated by the census in 1900, one-third paid no dividends whatever after their formation and another one-third paid no dividends to the holders of common stock.

As an indication of the profits obtained by the successful trust promoter may be cited the testimony given before the Industrial Commission in the case of the Tin Plate Trust, stating that this promoter realized from $2,000,000 to $3,000,000 profit from the undertaking. When to this is added the profit obtained by the owners of the constituent plants, which were usually taken over by the trust at an exorbitant valuation, it is clear that the stimulus of financial gain was probably stronger in many cases than that of economy in production. The bill was of course paid in most cases by the investing public, which absorbed large amounts of industrials in the years of their active promotion.

MISCELLANEOUS CAUSES OF TRUSTS

Other causes have sometimes been adduced to explain the growth of combinations, such as the tariff and railroad freight discriminations, but these are too local in their influence to explain adequately the world-wide movement toward combination. Trusts exist in free-trade England, and in Germany where freight discriminations on the state-owned railroads are practically unknown. It is, however, true that in the United States both these factors have been of decisive importance in building up certain powerful trusts. The conservative report of the Industrial Commission states as follows:

There can be no doubt that in early times special favors from railroads were a prominent factor, probably the most important factor, in building up some of the largest combinations. The receipt of discriminating favors from railroads has been conceded repeatedly by representatives of the combinations themselves.

The Standard Oil, beef, coffee, steel, and other trusts may be cited as illustrations. In the matter of the tariff Mr. Havemeyer's statement that "the mother of all trusts is the customs tariff law" may be set down as the rather peevish utterance of a disappointed beneficiary; but there is no doubt that combination has been made easier behind the tariff wall, for instance, the sugar trust itself, the leather, steel, tin plate, and others.

Still other causes which have aided the trust movement are such factors as patents, the widening of the market, and fluctuation in industry. That patents have aided the formation of trusts is well illustrated in the telephone business. All governmental privileges are apt to favor the combination movement. Through the invention and practical application of improvements in transportation, refrigeration, communication, credit facilities, and so on, not only have opportunities been created for the formation of trusts in these lines, but the markets of the world

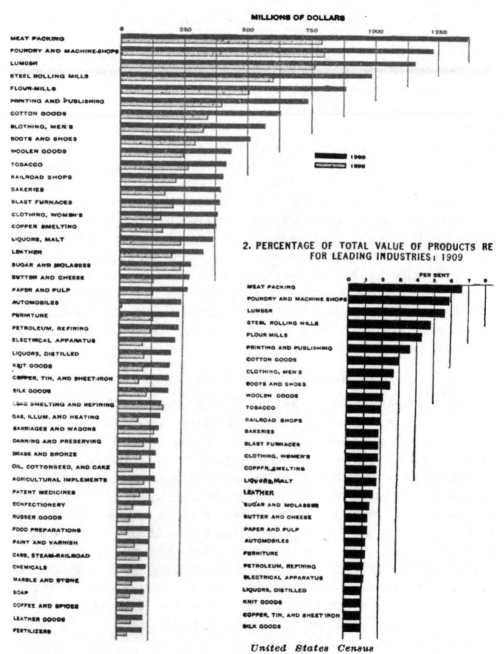

FIG. 8.—These Tables Show the Relative Importance of Industries in Relation to the Trust Movement

were opened and invited selling on a large scale. Marketing often lends itself even better to centralized control than production. For this reason the expansion of the market must be counted as one of the factors in the modern trust movement.

Fluctuations in industry usually aid combinations in competitive businesses in two ways. In the first place they are apt to force the weaker concerns to the wall, while the stronger can best survive the irregularities in supply and demand. Following the adjustment which takes place after every fluctuation, the stronger businesses are better able to take advantage of new opportunities and thus increase their economic position. In the next place fluctuations in industry encourage trusts because only by widespread co-operation can the amount of production be regularly adapted to the demand, and the demoralizing effects of over-production avoided. In this connection one should remember that the essence of all monopoly is control over supply.

Economic Effects of Trusts

Let us now turn to some of the effects of industrial combinations, which we may classify according as they bear upon competitors and producers of raw materials, labor, and consumers. As the number of competitors is reduced, the fierceness of competition among those remaining in the field is greatly increased, for the value of the prize to the successful enterprise is correspondingly greater. It is not surprising therefore that at times this rivalry should have assumed unethical if not actually illegal forms. The practice by some trusts of fixing prices below cost at some strategic point in order to crush out a troublesome competitor, and then correspondingly raising them elsewhere so as not to sustain any loss, is serious because so subtle. Professor John B. Clark regards this as so serious an evil that he would have the Constitution amended in order that power might be given the federal government to prevent it.

The producers of raw materials, such as cattlemen, crude oil and coal producers, sugar and tobacco growers, and others, complain that the prices at which they sell their products are dictated to them by the trusts, which are practically the sole purchasers of what they have produced. They claim that prices are depressed to the lowest point possible and that every gain from increase of demand goes into the pockets of the trust managers. It may of course be answered that the trust cannot depress prices below the point at which a living profit can be secured by the producer of the raw material or he will stop producing; but there is no doubt that the monopoly power possessed by the trust in such cases will sometimes be used to the disadvantage of those for whose product it alone offers a market.

Trusts and Labor

The effects upon labor of the organization of capital in combined industries and under centralized control are more complex. As trusts have superseded single corporations because this mode of industrial organization was more economical, we must expect to find that one of the economies was the displacement of labor. The discharge of traveling salesmen has already been spoken of; with the consolidation of various plants under one control other high-priced men were let go—managers, superintendents, etc. The same thing was true at the other end of the industrial scale and thousands of workmen, usually the least efficient and capable, were deprived of work. The natural consequences of these combinations and economies were not clearly apparent at the time, because they were happily coincident with a period of business expansion and prosperity which reabsorbed into the industrial organism most of the displaced workers.

Another phase of the relation between trusts and labor is that of their effect upon wages. In general it may be said that there are only two sources out of which an increase of wages can be paid, and these are the profits of the business organizer and manager or the increased product of the business itself. Of these two only the latter can serve as a permanent source of higher wages. Now it is pretty evident that labor has not been in a position to force the trust magnates to forego their profits. On the other hand, wages in industries carried on by industrial combinations have risen, and it must therefore have been because there was more produced and consequently more to be divided. If the inefficient workers were discharged and only the best ones retained by the trusts, here is one explanation of why they could afford to pay high wages—they paid more because they got more done. As yet labor has not admitted that it is unable to cope with these industrial combinations; it has demanded, however, that it be allowed to combine on a national scale and to bargain collectively with combined capital on behalf of united labor.

Monopoly Control and Prices

The discussion of the effects of trusts upon the consumer leads at once to the discussion of their effects upon prices, for it is through the agency of price that the trust touches the ordinary man. The advantages claimed by trust organizers are economies of production and lowered cost; but the vital question to the consumer is whether lowered cost increases profits or reduces prices. On this point the Industrial Commission reaches the following conclusion:

In most cases the combination has exerted an appreciable power over prices, and in practically all cases it has increased the margin between raw materials and finished products. Since there is reason to believe that the cost of production over a period of years has lessened, the conclusion is inevitable that the combinations have been able to increase their profits.

Moreover the power over prices was greatest during certain periods when the control of the combinations was greatest. The problem therefore resolves itself into the question: Are trusts monopolies? While a categorical answer cannot be given to this, it may safely be affirmed that all trusts try to be monopolies. Nor is it necessary to control absolutely the production, sale, or purchase of a commodity in order to exercise monopoly power; the control of 50 or 60 per cent may suffice to secure virtual monopoly. The purpose of a monopoly is so to fix the price that it will obtain the maximum net profit. It is conceivable that this result may be attained by lowering the monopoly price below the point of the competitive price, but this is unusual. In general a monopoly price has meant a high price, and a high price has meant a restriction of the output. Where that has been the result of trust control, society has been injured, for not only has it not shared in the economies of production, but it actually gets less and has to pay more than it would have done under competition.

It may be said, however, that even in the case of the greatest monopoly there is always the specter of potential competition threatening its profits, while the possibility of substituting some other commodity for the monopolized article protects the consumer from too great

extortion and keeps the price within limits. Absolute
control over price is never exercised by any monopoly.
Nevertheless, we may fairly conclude, in the words of
Henry D. Lloyd, that "monopoly is business at the end
of its journey"; control over prices is the object of
combination.

MONOPOLY AND INDIVIDUAL OPPORTUNITY

There remains to be considered another charge of monopoly which has been brought against the trust, the monopoly of opportunity or the suppression of individual
initiative. It is no longer possible, it is claimed, for the
man of small means, even with good talents, to engage in
business for himself; he must accept some subordinate
position in a corporation where his individuality is
checked and his power of initiative does not find free
play. So far as this is true it would seem to be the result
not so much of the trust movement as of large-scale production. We have seen that the tendency of machine production is to enlarge the business unit and to call for the
investment of constantly larger amounts of capital in up-
to-date establishments. Some writers even point out that
the average business man who engages in business on his
own account fails, and that he should therefore be grate-
ful if more efficient producers offer him a remunerative
and steady salaried position. Without insisting upon
this point, we may remark that there are still large fields
of enterprise lying outside the area of monopolistic
control.

Large-scale production is best adapted to articles that can be
turned out in large quantities according to uniform patterns
and standards; individual initiative is still free in those lines of
production that call for artistic ability or appeal to individual

tastes, or which, like agriculture, are dependent upon variable conditions.[3]

Monopoly Evils

There are, however, other evils connected with trust organization and management that are more easily remediable and that call for legislative regulation. "The evils of combination, remedied by regulative legislation," concludes the report of the Industrial Commission,[4] "come chiefly from two sources: (1) the more or less complete exercise of the power of monopoly; (2) deception of the public through secrecy or false information." Various remedies have been suggested to meet the first class of evils, those of monopoly, generally in the direction of strengthening the powers of the federal government. We have however no lack of legislation on this subject already. Thirty-four states and territories have passed anti-trust laws, and the federal Anti-Trust Law of 1890 explicitly provides that "every contract, combination in the form of a trust or otherwise, or conspiracy in restraint of trade or commerce among the several states, or with foreign nations, is hereby declared illegal." The severe restrictive measures of the states have been largely nullified by the loose legislation of three or four "charter-granting" states, in which 95 per cent of all the trusts have accordingly been chartered, while the federal enactments have been found very difficult to enforce. It is not easy to define or to prove monopoly or conspiracy in restraint of trade.

The second class of evils has been met by statutes requiring publicity and more definitely fixing the responsibility of corporation officials. Such measures of control

[3] Bogart, *Economic History of the United States*, p. 412.
[4] Vol. XIX, p. 645.

must be the first step toward intelligent regulation and are to be commended as thoroughly reasonable. The establishment of the federal Bureau of Corporations with power to "investigate" industrial corporations engaged in interstate commerce has already led to the publication of some valuable reports. We must first proceed along the lines of publicity and intelligent information before we attempt more drastic remedies. The monopoly evils of trusts will probably be controlled more and more by state and national industrial commissions with powers similar to those of the Interstate Commerce Commission. The federal Trade Commission, organized in 1915, has been created for this purpose.

TEST QUESTIONS

1. Account for the development of the combination movement in modern industry.

2. Enumerate the phases through which combinations for the purpose of fixing prices have passed.

3. What have been some of the chief causes of the trust movement?

4. How does the combination movement bring about economies in marketing?

5. What is meant by integration? What has been its influence upon the combination movement?

6. What are some of the benefits to be derived from the trust movement?

7. How is the trust problem related to the labor problem?

8. What are the peculiar dangers which result from monopoly in industry?

9. How are governments attempting to control the monopoly evil?

10. What is a holding company? How is centralized control secured through this device?

CHAPTER VI

SPECULATION AND CRISES

SPECULATIVE RISKS IN INDUSTRY

An unavoidable element of risk enters into all modern business. In the old handicraft stage of industry goods were made upon order; demand preceded supply very definitely, and there was little possibility of mistakes in production. Nowadays, as we have seen, production is for a distant and often uncertain market. It is carried on by machine methods and roundabout processes; sometimes the result is a very remote one and the uncertainty of success is correspondingly great. Production is not based upon order, but upon a forecast of the possible demand, upon a future market.

Chance and change are inseparable from productive enterprise—natural chances from the elements, political changes, such as war or unfavorable legislation, industrial mistakes, sickness or death of oneself or others, and economic changes, like the invention of a new machine or a change in fashion. These are the unavoidable incidents in industry and are not under the control of the individual business. Some of them, however, are so regularly recurrent that they can be foretold on a large scale for any industrial society and can be guarded against by insurance. Everyone recognizes the desirability of having such risks as those of fire, shipwreck, lightning, death, etc., assumed by certain individuals or companies who make a business of such risk-taking. A small premium is paid by the individual for protection against anxiety due to fear of mischance, and he is able to devote his whole energies and capital to his business; the insurance company has specialized in this one department and by equalizing the chances over a wide field has practically eliminated them. In doing this it performs a service of recognized and undoubted social value.

FUNCTION OF THE SPECULATOR

There is another kind of risk-taking, the social utility of which is not at first sight so clear. Among the chances of productive enterprise are those due to the rise and fall in the prices of the raw materials, the labor, and the finished product between the time when the process of production is begun and the time when it is completed. Every farmer, every manufacturer, every student even who invests capital in his own education, is to some extent a speculator. Along certain lines he can protect himself by insurance, but that is not possible in all. Is there no way, then, by which he can guard himself against price fluctuations and assure himself of the legitimate gains of his business? This, it may be answered, is the function of the speculator in modern business, and in performing this service he is benefiting society in much the same way as the insurance company does. We must, however, clearly distinguish between legitimate and illegitimate speculation; we are discussing only the former.

SERVICES OF STOCK AND PRODUCE EXCHANGES

One way in which the speculative risk attaching to price fluctuations is reduced for the manufacturer and assumed by the speculator is by the establishment of a continuous open market, like the stock and produce exchanges. If a miller, for instance, engages to deliver flour a year hence and expects to begin milling in six months, he must know at what price he can buy his wheat when he needs it, or his anticipated gain may be turned into a loss by an unexpected rise in the price of wheat. He is able, however, to buy a future in wheat on the produce exchange from some broker who makes a specialty of this business. He buys his needed wheat now for delivery six months hence, and on the basis of this price is able to accept an order for his flour a year from now, allowing himself a fair profit as a miller but wholly eliminating the speculative risk of price fluctuations. Or a building contractor, before making an estimate of the cost of erecting a structure, will secure options at definite prices from dealers on the materials he will require. So, too, in the iron and steel business it is customary for manufacturers to contract in advance for materials at the same time that they accept orders for the delivery of the finished products.

In all these cases the business of dealing in futures is assumed by a particular class of people who have developed a special skill and ability in forecasting price variations and who can do so very accurately. It is not a matter of luck or chance, but the result of wide knowledge and careful study. "To foretell the price of wheat one must know the rainfall in India, the condition of the crop in Argentina, must be in touch as nearly as possible with every unit of supply that will come into the market." Sometimes the speculators make mistakes, but they are certainly less apt to do so than men who are without their special talent and training.

BENEFITS OF SPECULATION

The social value of this service lies in the equalization of demand and supply between the present and future that is thereby effected. Let us take as an illustration the case of the miller cited above. If the price of wheat is high at the time he accepts the order for flour, he will be inclined to charge a high price. But the wheat broker, foreseeing that there is going to be an abundant crop six months hence, engages to sell him his wheat for future delivery at a low price, and he is thereby enabled to sell his flour at a lower price. At the same time the price of the wheat on hand at the present time, instead of being held and sold at famine prices, is consumed for present needs at moderate prices.

The operations of the wheat brokers in such a case have a very steadying influence on prices, preventing the oscillation between very high prices in times of scarcity and very low prices in times of glut. It must be admitted that dealings in futures are highly speculative; "but it must be remembered that it is not merely the dealings in futures, but the future itself, that is uncertain. If such dealings can be confined to the men most competent to make accurate predictions, their tendency will clearly be to lessen the uncertainties of business."[1]

But closely connected with legitimate speculation or risk-taking by a specialized and trained class, there is, as our stock and produce exchanges are actually conducted, a large amount of illegitimate speculation, and to this we may now turn for a brief consideration.

ILLEGITIMATE SPECULATION

The facilities offered by the open markets on the exchanges and the practice of dealing in futures are taken advantage of by many who, without any special training or opportunities of knowing the market, simply bet on the

[1] Seager, *Introduction to Economics*, p. 176.

price movements. Brokers are willing to buy and sell produce or stocks for their customers if the latter will put up with them a margin of about 10 per cent to protect them from loss. It is therefore possible for a person with little capital and no knowledge to speculate on a margin, buying what he does not want and selling what he does not own. In practice it is impossible to distinguish between those dealings in which actual delivery is intended (legitimate speculation) and those in which no such delivery is contemplated (gambling), and consequently most efforts to regulate transactions on the exchanges have failed to accomplish their purpose. The purification of their methods would seem to lie with the members of such exchanges themselves.

The contention has often been made that these fictitious transactions in such commodities as wheat or corn or cotton create an artificial reduction in prices, since the professional gambler usually sells short or "bears" the market, and that this injuriously affects the farmer. This is manifestly untenable, since every fictitious sale must be balanced by a fictitious purchase. What actually takes place is simply a bet between the two parties to such a transaction on the actual course of prices and of itself does not affect prices, except in the unusual case of a "corner." There is, however, great possibility of evil in the presence of a crowd of uninformed speculators, for they can greatly increase the power of an unscrupulous operator who can persuade them to follow his lead. Their presence, too, increases the temptation to such a man to rig the market. Under present conditions the abuses of speculation are more in evidence than the economic advantages. How to confine speculation to the small group of risk-takers who have special training and aptitude for it, and to prevent gambling on the stock and produce exchanges is one of the economic problems of the day.

CRISES

One of the most striking phenomena of modern industry is the frequent and violent convulsions of business known as "crises." They are characteristic of all commercially advanced countries and are generally most marked in those countries which are most advanced. They are a product of modern methods of capitalistic production and are essentially a phenomenon of the nineteenth century. A crisis in its last analysis is the result of a lack of adjustment between production and consumption, due primarily to mistakes in production. It is significant that crises usually occur in periods of business prosperity, when credit is easy, prices high, and employment general. Such a period of business prosperity and rising credit may have been begun by a series of good harvests. The demand for manufactured commodities increases, prices rise, manufacturers enlarge their factories or engage in new enterprises, wages and profits go up. Many speculators, seeing the rise and thinking it will continue, borrow money to buy goods, with the expectation of selling again at a profit. Credit operations are expanded to a dangerous extent, and when at last a shock to confidence occurs the house of cards collapses and a painful liquidation and readjustment of industry ensues. The state of trade, in the words of Lord Overstone, "revolves apparently in an established cycle. First we find it in a state of quiescence—next improvement, growing confidence, prosperity, excitement, over-trading, convulsion, pressure, stagnation, distress, ending again in quiescence."

ANALYSIS OF A CRISIS

The immediate occasion of a crisis is always a shock to credit or confidence. Such a shock, begun perhaps by the failure of a bank or merchant, creates a demand for ready money. No one is sure that his neighbor will remain solvent. Everyone accordingly tries to secure himself against loss by enlarging his cash reserve and thus lessens the supply for others. Now modern industry is carried on by means of credit. There is at no one time enough money in the country to meet all obligations expressed in terms of money. Considerably over three-fourths of the larger commercial transactions in the United States are carried on by means of credit. If everyone tries at the same time to get actual cash, there is simply not enough money in the country to go around. This increase of demand and diminution in the supply of money force up the interest rate on short-time loans. Money—actual cash—is needed by many people to meet immediate engagements and they are willing to pay almost any price for it. In the last panic the rates for call money went up to over 100 per cent and in many cities in the United States clearing-house certificates and other substitutes for money were issued for use in ordinary retail trade.

But even at these very high rates money can often not be borrowed. Many merchants and manufacturers are compelled to sell their goods at a sacrifice in order to obtain it. Vast quantities of goods and securities are thrown on the market just when investors and consumers feel least able to purchase. The result is a fall in prices. Such a fall in prices lowers profits. Enterprises have been started and engagements made on the supposition that prices would continue at the old high level.

When they fall it is impossible to pay interest out of current earnings. Foreclosures and readjustments take place. There is a general liquidation and reorganization of industry. When interest contracts have been adjusted, then the effect on wages begins to be felt. As long as a manufacturer is struggling to maintain his credit he will keep his factory going, but when he has failed and perhaps been foreclosed, then the factory stops. Men are thrown out of work, and wages—the price of labor—fall. Labor troubles usually mark the end of such a period of readjustment.

RECURRENCE OF CRISES

This stage marks the end of the crisis and the beginning of a period of depression or "hard times," which continues for a longer or shorter period. The panic of 1893 was followed by a long-continued depression which lasted until 1897, a period which was marked by low prices and slack work. In 1898 began a revival of business and an era of marked prosperity set in which continued for almost ten years, interrupted only slightly by a "Wall Street panic" in 1903. In October, 1907, a severe crisis occurred, recovery from which, however, was remarkably rapid. The periodicity which has attended crises in the past is so marked—occurring as they have at intervals of about ten years—that many writers consider them inevitable. As the easiest way to answer this question we may take up three main theories as to the causes of crises.

THE SUN-SPOT THEORY OF CRISES

A much quoted, but now generally discredited, theory is that of W. S. Jevons, a noted English economist, who ascribed crises to sun-spots. Every ten years and a fraction there occur outbursts of electrical and heat energy on the sun, which we call sun-spots. These result in increased heat waves, which affect the crops on the earth, causing enlarged harvests in Europe and the United States and drought and famine in India and the tropics. The large harvests and good prices start a wave of prosperity and speculation, which culminates inevitably in a panic and depression, until a recurrence of the heat phenomenon starts the cycle again. The theory states some undoubted facts, but no causal connection between sun-spots and crises can be traced, as the latter are too irregular and the two do not always coincide. Were this theory true, crises would be beyond human control.

THE OVER-PRODUCTION THEORY OF CRISES

A second theory, or group of theories, is that which attributes crises to over-production. Under modern conditions of industry a small group of men direct industry and determine what shall be produced. They try to estimate future demand and to adjust production to consumption, but they often make mistakes. They divert capital into unproductive industries, they produce the wrong things and create a comparative glut in certain lines, and when they cannot sell their goods at a profitable price they fail and precipitate a crisis. Industry must then be reorganized and frequently control be put in the hands of other men.

A variation has been given this theory by the socialists, under the leadership of Rodbertus, who insist that the reason that there is over-production is because of the institution of private property. Since the capitalists own all the tools of production they pay the laborers only starvation wages. The latter cannot possibly buy all that is produced and commodities consequently heap up in the warehouses until they are thrown upon the market to be sold at any price. Then a panic occurs and a readjustment of production takes place.

THE CREDIT THEORY OF CRISES

The last of these theories regards a crisis as essentially due to a failure of credit. It is seen that a large part of modern industry is carried on with borrowed capital, by roundabout processes, and for a distant market and not upon order. That is, the success of a business depends upon its ability to sell its goods when produced. Now the aggregate volume of transactions that can be carried on in a year, so runs the theory, depends upon the efficiency of the credit system—that is, in general, upon the freedom with which banks are willing to loan money to people who engage to repay it in the future out of their ventures. If for any reason the banks reduce this accommodation the amount of business that can be transacted upon borrowed capital is lessened. Either some transactions must stop or prices must fall. Either of these events causes commercial disaster. The contraction of credit makes it impossible to get the goods into the right hands, and so we have the phenomenon of over-production in a great many lines. As exchange and transportation have developed and markets widened, crises have become more universal. According to this theory, they are inseparably connected with the use of credit and can be controlled only by a more careful granting of credit by the banks to industrial managers.

Another phase of the credit theory is presented by those who insist that the cause of crises is the rhythmic over-estimation of the profits to be secured out of certain lines of production, or their over-capitalization. The new enterprises are financed by the banks on the basis of this mistaken over-capitalization, their organizers engage to pay rates of interest which they cannot earn, and the crash inevitably follows. This is often called the over-capitalization theory, and it is essentially psychological in its character.

There is no doubt as to the truth contained in this last theory. It helps to explain the rhythmic periodicity of crises. After every period of business depression confidence revives and hope is renewed; over-estimation of the success of new ventures is inevitable. Then follows a mistaken investment of capital in certain lines of production, as in railroads in 1884, and a relative over-production of certain commodities at profitable prices. The true explanation seems to be found in a combination of the over-production and over-capitalization theories.

CAN CRISES BE PREVENTED?

The practical problem that presents itself in this connection is the question as to whether it is possible to prevent the recurrence of crises. In view of the explanation just given it would seem that they must be regarded as unpreventable as long as industry is carried on under the competitive capitalistic system of production and the modern credit system. Moreover crops differ in amount from year to year and probably always will. Human production and human genius are unequal. Crises may be regarded as the price a progressive society pays for its advance, and they may be expected to recur pretty regularly at periodic intervals. Their disastrous effects may, however, be greatly lessened by wise currency legislation, by greater care in granting credit, and by greater wisdom in the direction of individual effort.

TEST QUESTIONS

1. What are some of the factors that make chance and change inseparable from modern industry?

2. How does the speculator reduce for the merchant the speculative risk attached to price fluctuations? Illustrate.

3. How do stock and produce exchanges assist the speculator in this function?

4. Explain the difference between legitimate speculation and gambling.

5. What is meant by a crisis?

6. Discuss the immediate occasion of a crisis.

7. Account for the recurring features of crises.

8. What was Jevons' sun-spot theory of crises?

9. Explain the overproduction theory of crises. Suggest an illustration from our own history that would seem to support this theory.

10. What are the essential characteristics of the credit theory of crises?

11. What theory of crises seems most reasonable to you?

12. What suggestions have you to make as to how crises may be prevented?

CHAPTER VII

THE MODERN WAGE SYSTEM

THE FACTORY SYSTEM AND LABOR

We have already characterized the modern system of industry as capitalistic, that is, as involving the use of expensive and complex machinery in factories under the control of the capitalist managers of industry. As we have seen, such a system has caused an enormous increase in the production of wealth; it has also raised the general standard of comfort and the level of wages and has relieved labor to a considerable extent of the deadly strain of hard manual toil that was characteristic of preceding systems.

The factory system, under which capitalistic production is now carried on, may also fairly be credited with other beneficial results. As steadiness and punctuality are essential, it has on the whole led to increased sobriety and temperance; the work in general is healthier, being performed under better sanitary conditions than under the old domestic system; the intellectual status of the workingman has been raised, as vastly more intelligence is required of a skilled machine operator than of the old-time hand laborer; and finally the general well-being of the working class has been improved, as they have shared in the larger production made possible by machine methods.

91

But, on the other hand, the new processes and methods have been accompanied by great abuses, though never so great in this country as in England. Long hours, the employment of women and children, the weakened economic position of the laborer, fluctuations in production, liability to be without employment, industrial accidents, the abolition of personal ties between employer and employe, the crowding of workmen into a small space to work by day, and their concentration in city tenements by night—these are some of the problems for which the factory system must be held responsible. The condition and position of labor have been vitally affected. So far we have considered mainly the problems connected with the organization and use of capital. We must now take up the various questions connected with the relation of labor to capital and to the capitalistic system of production.

THE WAGE-EARNING CLASS

One of the most vital factors in the situation—which we must frankly admit at the start—is the existence in modern industrial society of a distinct wage-earning class. It is perfectly obvious that under present conditions of production great capital or great ability is necessary in order to become the manager of an industrial enterprise. Most laborers do not possess either the one or the other of these, and although there are fortunate examples of industrial leaders who have risen from the ranks, the general rule is, once a wage-earner, always a wage-earner.

The number of those who can achieve industrial independence is moreover growing smaller as business becomes more specialized and centralized. The laborer therefore belongs to a class which is rapidly developing what the German socialists call "class-consciousness," that is, the feeling that he belongs to a'distinct industrial group with interests different from and often antagonistic to those of other groups or classes. In his struggles with employers over wages this antagonism of immediate aims obscures the deeper mutuality and interdependence of their really complementary interests and not infrequently leads to a feeling of hostility, finding expression in strikes and labor agitation.

DEPENDENCE OF THE WAGE-EARNER

In the transition to the factory system Mr. John A. Hobson [1] points out that the position of the laborer has been one of increasing dependence in the following five important points:

First, ownership of material. At first the worker owned this and made it into the finished product, but now he has only a passing interest in a small part of the process of working it up.

Second, ownership of tools. He retained these up to the time of the introduction of machinery, but now seldom owns them.

Third, control of productive power. With the displacement of hand labor and muscular power by steam-driven machinery, he no longer owns even this.

Fourth, relations between workers and employers. They were formerly on an equality; under the guild system the master and the apprentice had the same social position; now the laborer has sunk in the scale, or the employer has risen, until the only bond between them is, as Carlyle said, the "cash nexus." A case was recently instanced where a workingman who had been

---

[1] *Evolution of Modern Capitalism*, p. 35.

working in a factory met his employer for the first time at the end of seventeen years.

Fifth, work-place. Until the establishment of the factory system this had always been the home; now it is the factory, and there is a complete divorcement between work and the home.

THE WAGE SYSTEM

Another characteristic of modern industry from the labor point of view is the existence not merely of a wage-earning class, but, more fundamental, of the wage system. President Hadley, of Yale University, writes as follows: [2]

It is characteristic of the modern industrial system that a laborer who owns no capital, though nominally free to do what he pleases, must actually find some property owner who will give him enough to keep him alive during the period which must elapse between the rendering of the labor and the sale of the finished product. Under such circumstances, the laborer almost inevitably submits to the direction of the property owner in deciding how his labor shall be applied. Laborers without capital must necessarily work on this basis; even those who have small amounts of capital habitually do so. Such advances of capital are known as wages.

Here we have the essence of the wage system in a nut shell. The laborer sells his labor to an employer for a stipulated wage. He has a commodity, his labor, consisting of a certain amount of strength and skill, which he is free to dispose of on the market to the best advantage, as the owner of any other commodity might do. Legally, labor is property.

[2] *Economics*, p. 121.

Owing, however, to the fact that all modern production requires capital, the only buyer of his labor is a capitalist, who directs the way in which the labor shall be applied. Such a condition, as well as some peculiarities of the commodity—labor, leaves the laborer, indeed, only nominally free. In theory the labor contract is a perfectly free contract, entered into voluntarily by both employer and wage-earner, and the courts have generally insisted that this theoretical freedom must be maintained. In practice various modifications of the theory have taken place. Legislation has been passed protecting laborers from bargaining away their rights, and trade unions have been formed to bargain collectively for a group of laborers. In the last analysis, however, the laborer must support himself by the sale of his labor; society guarantees him neither a living nor even the right to work. He is a bargainer in a competitive industrial world and he must assume the responsibility of providing for himself and his family by securing work. Just what is involved in such a statement is perhaps best brought out by comparing the modern wage system with previous systems of labor.

THE EVOLUTION OF THE WAGE CONTRACT

The first historical system of labor, aside from that in the family, was that of slaves. In this case the labor was forced and, being given under coercion, was probably very inefficient; but the laborer was at least assured of a minimum of food, clothes, and shelter. Slavery was the main source of manual labor in the ancient world, and did not disappear in England until the eleventh century. The feudal system of the Middle Ages was characterized by serfdom, according to which the laborer was bound to the soil and was compelled to render his lord

certain services. Gradually serfdom was broken down
and the wage system took its place, although remnants
of serfdom remained in England until the eighteenth
century.

Four centuries before this, however, the disintegration
of the feudal society had already begun, the serfdom of
the agricultural laborer was commuted into regular
money payments, and the artisan bought or otherwise
secured his freedom from feudal exactions. In the towns
industry was regulated by the guilds, and while at first
they were distinctly beneficial, in time they became monopolistic and oppressive. Power was lodged in the
hands of the wealthy traders and merchants and they leg-
islated in their own behalf against the growing class of
laborers, as did the wealthy landowners against the agricultural laborers. The Statute of Laborers and other
acts sought to fix wages and to prevent the freedom of
the laborer in moving about or choosing his own occupation. Not indeed until the nineteenth century were the
last of these old regulative laws repealed and the modern labor contract recognized in law and practice as a
free contract. "The growth of labor," says Brentano,
"has been from the system of authority to the system of
contract." The system of authority, by which rates of
wages, length of apprenticeship, and other details of industry were fixed by some superior authority, was found
to be restrictive, uneconomic, and unjust, and it gave way
to the principle of economic freedom. According to the
newer theory, first given effective voice in 1776 by Adam
Smith, the individual should be left to himself, as he
knows his own interest better than does the most enlightened government. The freest scope was given to the
powers of individuals and each was to be the unlimited
master of himself and his possessions.

PUBLIC REGULATION OF LABOR CONDITIONS

It has since been found necessary, however, to modify both the theory and practice of this extreme individualism in order to protect the interests of various classes of society, especially the laborer. The legal theory still is that "today the labor contract is perfectly free: either side may make whatever contract he can get the other side to sign. Not only this, but either side may freely combine to demand any form of contract from the other side, as mere combinations alone are now made perfectly legal." [3] In practice, however, this complete freedom has been greatly modified by factory acts, acts restricting the hours and conditions of employment of women and children, anti-truck acts, laws providing for weekly payments, guarding of machinery, limiting the hours of labor, and on the other hand prohibiting intimidation and molesting. For the most part these laws have applied to women and children, who are thought less capable of guarding their own interests, and to a much less degree to labor contracts made by men, who have been considered better able to make equal contracts with employers. But concerning certain conditions of employment it has been realized that even adult males are not capable of securing equitable bargains, and along these lines the nominal freedom of the labor contract has been decidedly abridged. The attitude of the courts toward such legislation shows that they have declared many laws unconstitutional on the ground that they infringe upon the right of free contract, but in the long run seem inclined to uphold as much of this restrictive legislation as seems necessary to obviate the undoubtedly evil results that flow from this real inequality of employer and laborer.

[3] Stimson, *Labor in its Relation to Law,* p. 51

It is a very vital and important practical economic
problem that presents itself in this connection. How far
shall we carry this regulative principle, or how far shall
we insist upon the principle of freedom? Many labor
leaders are again asking for an effectual control of the labor contract, not by the action of trade unions, but by the
direct legislation of the state. What shall be our attitude
to this demand? Before we can fairly answer this question we must consider somewhat more fully the character
of the bargain that takes place between an employer and
an individual workman and the nature of the commodity
that the laborer has to sell.

LABOR'S BARGAINING POWER

It has already been stated that the commodity which
the laborer brings upon the market is his labor, that is,
himself, his time, and his energies. But these wares are
peculiar and differ in several important respects from ordinary marketable commodities. In the first place labor
is like a perishable commodity which must be sold at once
if the owner is not to incur loss. The laborer has usually
little if any capital with which to support himself in case
he cannot find work, and he may be compelled to make a
forced sale of his labor, that is, to accept unduly low
wages. In this respect then he is at a disadvantage in
bargaining with his employer. A second peculiarity of
the sale of labor is that the laborer and his work are inseparable. The seller of an ordinary commodity disposes
of it absolutely when he makes a sale.

It matters nothing to the seller of bricks whether they are to
be used in building a palace or a sewer; but it matters a great
deal to the seller of labor, who undertakes to perform a task of
given difficulty, whether or not the place in which it is to be

done is a wholesome and a pleasant one, or whether or not his associates will be such as he cares to have.

The person who buys this labor necessarily directs the application of it to the task in hand, and thus controls very largely the place, the sanitary and social conditions, the hours, the character, and safety of the work. In the third place the superior knowledge and intelligence of the employers give them an advantage in bargaining with their employes, while the reluctance of employers to "spoil the labor market" often prevents that freedom of competition which is supposed to secure to the laborer his full share of the product he helps to produce.

NECESSITY OF PROTECTIVE LEGISLATION

In view of these facts we may fairly conclude that workmen are inferior to employers as bargainers and that protective legislation is necessary in order to put them on a real equality.

When laborers have to make a forced sale of their labor, their freedom of contract is more nominal than real. When women and children stand individually before the manager of hundreds of thousands of capital, it is possible that there may be little freedom and less equality in the contract by which they sell their services.[4]

It is clear that between two parties of such unequal knowledge, resources, and ability as a laborer and his employer the labor contract cannot be entirely free and equal. While trade unions, by combining isolated workmen into formidable and unified groups, have immeasurably increased their bargaining strength, yet legisla-

[4] Bullock, *Introduction to the Study of Economics*, p. 428.

tion has also been found necessary to remedy the disadvantages already enumerated. It is realized that "there is no greater inequality than the equal treatment of unequals."

In the opening chapter of this book attention was called to the fact that economic freedom or liberty was one of the corner stones of our modern industrial society. But freedom can best be secured by securing equality and responsibility. Factory legislation and labor laws are designed to correct the inequalities imposed by nature or involved in the very nature of capitalistic production. Direct interference by the state in the freedom of contract is justified as leading to a more real and certain equality and liberty. But while we may thoroughly approve the principle of labor legislation it is difficult to know at what point we should stop.

A leading American authority on the law of labor has stated [5] that "the industrial laborer at least is beginning to be a privileged class in the law." On the other hand, it was possible for Disraeli to say as late as 1875, after the passage of the Employers and Workmen Act by the British Parliament, that "for the first time in the history of this country employer and employed sit under equal laws." So recently were the legal disabilities removed under which the English workmen had suffered up to this time.[6] The pendulum has swung so rapidly and so far in labor's direction in the last generation that it is a fair question how far it will, or should, continue to go.

[5] Stimson, *Labor in Its Relation to Law*, p. 71.
[6] Ruegg, *Law of Employer and Workman in England*, p. 99.

TEST QUESTIONS

1. How is the modern wage system dependent upon the factory system in industry?

2. What do we mean by a distinct wage-earning class? To what problems does it give rise?

3. Name five points which Mr. Hobson gives to show that in the transition to the factory system, the position of the laborer has been one of increasing dependence.

4. What is President Hadley's explanation of the wage system?

5. Why has the wage contract been subject to severe questioning during the last quarter of a century?

6. What does Brentano mean by the sentence, "The growth of labor has been from the system of authority to the system of contract"?

7. How has the extreme individualism of Adam Smith's theory been modified?

8. What are the three peculiarities in the sale of labor?

9. Why has protective labor legislation become a necessity?

CHAPTER VIII

LABOR ORGANIZATIONS AND COLLECTIVE BARGAINING

CAUSES OF LABOR ORGANIZATIONS

As modern capitalistic production caused the growth of a distinct wage-earning class and brought about a sharp separation between employers and laborers, and as the latter were thrown upon their own resources under the prevailing theories of free competition and free contract, it was inevitable that they should organize to secure their interests as a class. The growth of labor organizations has been greatest in those countries where the laborer has been forced to depend mostly upon his own efforts for protection and improvement, namely, in England and the United States. On the continent of Europe, on the other hand, where the individual has been accustomed to look to the government for the redress of industrial grievances, there has been a much less vigorous and spontaneous development of such organizations. They are a product of the nineteenth century and had their origin in modern machine production.

TYPES OF LABOR ORGANIZATIONS

The growth of labor organizations in the United States has proceeded hand in hand with the industrial development of this country, and has been especially rapid since the Civil War. Two distinct types of trade unions may be noted: the local and the national (or international) unions. The former, which comprises members who live and work in the same locality, is the primary unit, and dates back to the beginning of the century. Each local union, even when subordinate to a national organization, is a self-governing unit and is absolutely democratic. Its relation to the national body has been well compared to that of one of our states to the United States. The first national union was not formed until 1850, but now these far surpass the locals in importance. Their government is representative, as they are made up of local unions.

The great majority of the national trade unions are bound together in the powerful federal organization, the American Federation of Labor. The membership of this body numbers about 1,800,000, while the railroad brotherhoods, which are not connected with it, claim about 335,000 more. Somewhat over 2,000,000 persons in the United States belong to labor organizations. This is about 10 per cent of the total working population or about 15 per cent of those engaged in trade and transportation, manufacturing, and mechanical pursuits. While this does not seem a very large proportion and is not as large as the membership of British trade unions, yet it must be remembered that they constitute on the whole the elite of the labor world and exercise an authority and power out of proportion to their numbers. Many other workmen who do not themselves belong to the unions follow their lead and are directly affected by their actions.

NATIONAL ORGANIZATIONS

Historically the two most important national organizations in this country have been the Knights of Labor and the American Federation of Labor, and they represent such different principles that it will be worth while

to describe them.   The Knights of Labor was organized
in 1869 as a local union of seven garment cutters and had
a meteoric career, counting a membership of 730,000 in
1886, the year of its greatest strength.   It was a national
amalgamation of mixed local assemblies composed of
workers of all trades who lived in the same locality.   It
held the theory that the interests of all members of the
laboring class are identical and must be cared for at the
same time, if possible, by political action, by co-operation,
and by education.   In 1886, however, it entered upon a
series of disastrous strikes; later it came into conflict
with trade unions which had not joined its ranks and
were opposed to its policies; and finally it became en-
tangled in politics.

As it lost in influence and strength its place was taken
by the American Federation of Labor, which was its very
opposite in organization and government.   This latter
body is a "confederation of trade and labor unions,"
each trade being organized separately into local unions
which are given great autonomy, these unions alone being represented in the national body.   Only matters of
general interest come before it, all local trade matters
being left to the local unions.

Objects and Methods of Labor Unions

More important than the history of labor organizations is a knowledge of their objects and methods.   The
primary purpose is of course to control the conditions of
labor and to substitute the principle of collective bargaining for individual contract.   As one of the most effective ways to secure this result they aim at a more or
less complete monopoly of the labor market.   This they
may do by bringing all workers in a trade within the
union or by preventing non-union men from working.

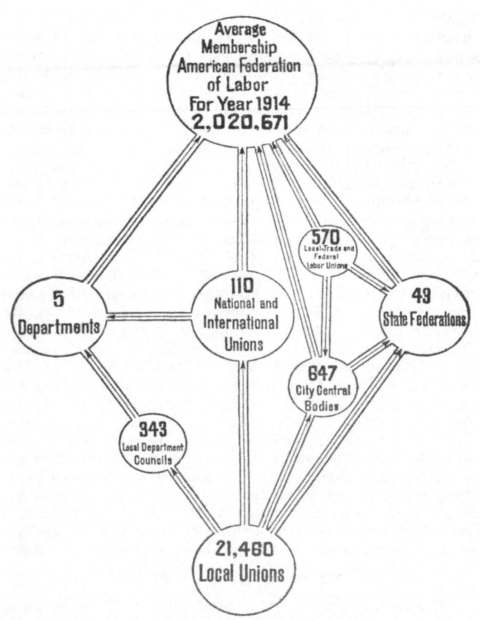

FIG. 9.—**Organization of the American Federation of Labor.** From Report
of Executive Council

The first of these is called the inclusive method,[1] and if successful makes the union the sole seller of the kind of labor controlled by its members. It is a monopoly of the laborers against the employers and is sought to be enforced by inducing men to join the union either by persuasion or coercion, the latter finding expression in the strikes against the employment of non-union men and the insistence upon the "closed shop."

The other form of monopoly consists in the exclusion of non-members from the trade and is a control of employment; this is a monopoly of a small group against their fellow-workmen. It is enforced by regulating the entrance to the trade, making it difficult or expensive, or by limiting the number of apprentices. Sometimes, as in the Chicago Building Trades in 1900, the workers have united with their employers by means of "exclusive agreements" to raise wages and prices of the finished products at the same time, and thus jointly to mulct the public. Such efforts to monopolize the labor market have their counterparts in the organization of capital, as we have seen. In practice such a labor monopoly has sometimes been used to improve and elevate conditions, just as sometimes a capitalistic monopoly has reduced prices below the competitive point. In general, however, we must condemn monopoly on principle in the competitive field and insist that freedom and opportunity be given to all on as equal terms as possible. Of the two forms of trade union monopoly, the former alone, which endeavors to make it all-comprehensive and to enforce union conditions generally, can be economically justified.

Standard Rate of Pay

"The establishment of a standard rate of wages may perhaps be said to be the primary object of trade union

---

[1] Report of Industrial Commission, Vol. XVII, p. 1.

policy. Without the standard rate the trade union, such as it is, could have no existence."[2] The purpose of the union is to substitute collective bargaining for individual agreements and thereby to improve the condition of its members. But if a single bargain is to determine the pay of a large number of men, there must be a common standard. In every employment on a large scale the men are necessarily grouped together and their pay is determined by a common rule. This is true even in non-union shops.

It is generally assumed that the standard rate of labor organizations means a uniform wage for each member, but this is not the case; it means rather a uniform rate of pay to all for the same performance. In the case of piecework, it could manifestly not mean anything else; but a large number of labor leaders object to piecework. They insist that a standard wage means a minimum wage, and that by the establishment of such a minimum the whole standard of efficiency and the plane of competition are raised, as the employers cannot then afford to hire any but competent workmen.

The question immediately presents itself: What is to become of the older or partially disabled men who are no longer able to earn the standard or minimum wage? In England they are practically guaranteed a subsistence by the union; in this country the union not infrequently exempts them from the provisions as to the standard wage. When the rule is enforced there is certainly a real hardship for these men.

But from the employers there comes the more serious complaint that the effect of the standard wage is to reduce to a dead level the efficient and the inefficient; that

[2] Report of Industrial Commission, Vol. XVII, p. xlii.

it is a maximum wage and that the efficient and industrious are prevented from earning more than a fixed amount. There is undoubtedly a great deal of truth in this charge; the man who hastens the pace is said to be taking "blood money," and sometimes a maximum wage is set which the members are forbidden to exceed. On the other hand it may fairly be said that while the union regulation of wages does tend to produce greater uniformity, the union rate is usually higher than the competitive rate would be, that is, wages are leveled up, not down; and finally that territorial variations make the local rate conform to local conditions.

REDUCTION IN WORKING HOURS

A reduction in the hours of labor has been even more strenuously urged by progressive labor leaders in the United States than an increase in wages. "Organize and control your trade and shorten your hours," is their contention, "and wages will take care of themselves." Their arguments in favor of a general shortening of the working day are twofold. In the first place, owing to the intensity and strain of work under modern machine methods, the worker cannot work efficiently more than eight or nine hours a day. The work is too exacting and the strain on the attention too great; it is a noticeable fact that most of the accidents in industrial establishments occur in the last hour or two of the working day. Not only that, but the laborer is entitled to his share of industrial progress in the form of more leisure, giving him time for a better family and social life, affording opportunity for intellectual improvement, and permitting the development of more rational and higher wants. With the improvement in the condition of the laboring classes will go the elevation of society as a whole.

The second argument in favor of shorter hours put forward by the trade unionist is economic rather than social. He argues that a ''reduction of hours will diminish the supply of labor in the market, and so will raise its price. It will make room for the unemployed, and so will remove the depressing influence of their competition.'' There is involved in this contention the familiar lump-of-labor argument of the trade unionist: There is just so much work to be done, and if some men do a little less there will be more for others. By shortening everyone's hours of labor, employment will be made more general and the work will be better distributed.

Now the economists in general have supported the trade unions in their demands for a shorter working day, but they have done so because they believed that the product of industry would not thereby be diminished. They have seen that when the hours of labor were reduced the laborer was less rapidly worn out physically, that he could work more rapidly for a short time, and that his increased leisure and pay, if rationally used, made him a more intelligent and efficient worker. In other words, a reduction in the hours of labor from 15 a day to 12, to 10, and even in some cases to 8, was not attended by a parallel reduction in the output, but the latter remained about the same. This is the great economic justification of the shorter working day, and as long as this can go on without materially affecting the product of industry it must be approved.

If, however, the latter is decreased there will be less to divide and then the relative disadvantages of a smaller dividend must be weighed against the advantages of increased leisure. Of course the point to which the number of hours can be reduced without lessening the product can be determined only by experiment, and will differ in different trades, but it is inevitable that until this point is reached the pressure of the trade unions for shorter working days, or for more holidays or half-holidays, will not be successfully resisted.

Turning now from theory to fact, we find that there has been a great improvement in the condition of labor in this respect. At the beginning of the nineteenth century the almost universal working day was, as McMaster tells us, from sun to sun. As factories grew up the habits of agricultural labor were carried over into industrial occupations, and working days of 16 and 18 hours were not uncommon. In 1903 the average length of the working day in the United States was 9.6 hours. This great reform may fairly be credited to the efforts of labor organizations themselves, for without their insistence and struggles it is unlikely that it would have been voluntarily granted by employers.

RESTRICTION OF OUTPUT

The limitation of output results almost necessarily from the above-mentioned practices of the unions. Reduction of hours, prohibition of piecework, and the standardization of wages all tend to restrict the output of the individual worker. But some of the unions have gone further and have directly limited the amount that could be produced during a given period by the laborer. This has been particularly true of British unions and is the subject of common complaint by English employers and writers, but illustrations may easily be found in the United States.

In Chicago in 1900 the lathers limited a day's work to twenty-five bundles of lath, for which they received $3; they had formerly done thirty-five bundles for a daily wage of $1.75.

Plasterers were limited to thirty square yards a day; the steam fitters were permitted to lay only ninety feet of steam pipe per day; but the plumbers had the most objectionable rules and restricted materially the amount of work that could be done in a day.[3]

These rules were defended by the unions on the ground that they were necessary in order to secure careful work and to prevent the "rusher" from setting the pace for a fair day's work.

The practice has not been uncommon, especially in the sweated trades, for an unscrupulous employer to pay a few particularly able workmen to put extra speed into their work and so set a pace that the other workmen would be compelled to maintain. This was especially objected to by the unions in the case of team work. They claimed that when all the workmen had come up to the new standard, particularly in piecework, the wages were reduced so that even by working at the higher rate of speed they could only make a fair wage. One of the rules of the Chicago carpenters' union provided that "any member guilty of excessive work or rushing on any job shall be reported and shall be subject to a fine of $5."

Whatever the excuse it is clear that such limitations cannot be economically justified. Not only does such dawdling undermine the industrial efficiency of the worker, but it is unfair to the employer. If the latter bargains for the union rate of wages and the normal working day, he is entitled to a full return of the laborer's best efforts. Otherwise there is no fairness in collective bargaining. "So far as labor leaders are con-

---

[3] Bogart, *The Chicago Building Trades Dispute* (Political Science Quarterly), Vol. XVI., p. 134; Commons, *Trade Unionism and Labor Problems*, p. 107.

cerned," said Mr. John Burns, the English trade unionist, "we are all strongly opposed to the restriction of production; we are all in favor of better and more conscientious work."

Laboring men have never been quite able to divest
themselves of their old antipathy to labor-saving machinery. They generally regard the introduction of a
new machine as a displacer of men, a creator of unemployment, a depresser of wages. Some unions have successfully resisted the introduction of machinery into their
trades, as the stone cutters in Chicago,[4] but in general
they have recognized the impossibility of this attitude.
They now demand that when machinery is introduced
it shall be operated by union men and their wages shall
be fixed so as to give the workers a share of the increased
production.

FRATERNAL BENEFITS OF LABOR UNIONS

The policies and methods of the trade unions thus far
discussed are those of a militant nature, but the fraternal
objects of these associations, though less conspicuous,
are none the less important. Labor organizations generally have insurance and benefit features, by which sick,
injured, or unemployed members are assisted. This is
particularly true of the English organizations, which
developed these features before the rise of the militant
new unionism. They often possess large funds and have
been rendered thereby more conservative and responsible. The educative effect of trade unionism among the
members is marked; some of them possess libraries and
all of them promote discussion and thought upon eco-

[4] Bogart, *The Chicago Building Trades Dispute* (Political Science Quarterly), Vol. XVI, p. 137.

nomic problems, while the administration of their affairs often gives valuable training. The older unions did much to encourage co-operation among their members, but today the tendency is to limit their activities to the essential one for which they are organized, namely, collective bargaining.

Collective Bargaining

Intelligent unionists realize that they can secure the various objects for which they strive only by substituting collective bargaining for contracts between employers and individual laborers. Where this plan is accepted by employers, representatives of the two sides agree upon wage scales, usually for a year; during this period the chief task of union officials is to see that the agreement is lived up to, and if possible to add to their membership and strengthen the union. In the United States relatively few trades have adopted this method as a general practice, the employers still being able to dictate wages and conditions of employment in most of them, while the unions are still struggling for recognition, if not for existence. In refusing to make collective bargains with the unions, employers insist that as they run all the risks, they must be permitted to manage their business as they see fit and without interference from the business agent of the union. In reply the unions insist that hours, wages, and conditions of employment are as much their business as that of the employer. The latter also urges that the trade unions as at present organized are too irresponsible and that before they ask for collective bargaining they should be incorporated, so that they could be sued for breach of contract if guilty of such. As yet, however, the unions have preferred their present position of irresponsibility and immunity and have almost invariably refused to be incorporated.   President Hadley, of Yale, writes: [5]

Strikes and Lockouts

In the minds of a large section of the public, labor unions are chiefly associated with strikes.   It is believed by many who ought to know better, that such organizations exist for the purpose of striking, and that if the organizations were suppressed, industrial peace would be secured.   The first of these ideas is a distorted one; the second is wholly unfounded.

Strikes are, however, a necessary concomitant of collective bargaining.   If the representatives of a union cannot come to terms with an employer, they may compel their members to refuse to sell their commodity, labor; such a concerted refusal to work is a strike.   The right to quit work has been regarded as a sacred one by trade unionists, but it involves social consequences of great importance.   For the workingman, it means loss of wages and demoralizing idleness; to the employer, idle capital, loss of profits, and depreciation of plant; and to the consuming public, inconvenience and annoyance together with curtailed production.   Quite aside from all acts of violence and lawlessness, by which they are too often accompanied, there is involved an enormous money waste.   According to a report of the Department of Labor, losses from strikes and lockouts in the United States from 1881 to 1900 amounted to $449,342,000, or an average loss per establishment of about $3,500.

Conciliation and Arbitration

The public is awakening to the realization that it suffers the greatest injury as the innocent third party to

[5] *Economics*, p. 353.

every industrial dispute, and it is insisting that the industrial peace be kept or more reasonable methods of settling
differences be found than a strike or lockout. Such a
method is found in conciliation and arbitration. In the
older and more strongly organized unions strikes are in-
frequent and methods of joint discussion and agreement
are increasingly resorted to. Boards of conciliation are
often provided for, which endeavor by means of conference and concession to prevent a dispute from arising;
they succeed best where both employers and employes
are organized. Should the dispute come to a head, however, provision is usually made for its reference to a
board of arbitration, which may be selected by the dis-
putants themselves or may be created by the state; in the
latter case the acceptance of the award may be voluntary
or compulsory.

In the United States most of the successful boards have
been those selected by the parties to the dispute; the state
boards have usually the power only of investigating the
causes of the trouble, but this in itself has proved of considerable value in more than one instance, notably in the
case of the Anthracite Coal Commission. Compulsory
arbitration is being given a thorough trial in Australasia
and seems to be meeting with success there. In this country, however, the trade unions are strongly opposed to
compulsory or enforced governmental arbitration. Writing of Great Britain, Mr. and Mrs. Webb assert that the
principle of arbitration, having been found inconsistent
with collective bargaining, is fast going out of favor. It
would seem from the experience of both England and the
United States that the chief virtue in these methods lies
in the habit of joint conference of the representatives of
labor and capital and the resulting conciliation.

TEST QUESTIONS

1. Why have labor organizations grown more rapidly in the United States and England than on the continent of Europe?

2. What are the two types of trade unions that prevail in the United States?

3. What were the essential features of the Knights of Labor? What caused the downfall of this organization?

4. What are the essential characteristics of the American Federation of Labor?

5. By what methods do labor organizations attempt to control the labor market?

6. Why do labor leaders generally object to piece, premium, and bonus systems of wage payment?

7. What arguments are put forth by the trade unionists in favor of shorter hours?

8. Give illustrations showing where unions have directly limited the amount of output.

9. What are some of the chief benefits which labor unions attempt to secure for their members?

10. What is the attitude of a great many employers in the United States toward collective bargaining?

11. For what reasons does labor occasionally resort to strikes and lockouts? How can strikes and lockouts be prevented?

12. Describe the method of settling an industrial dispute by conciliation.

CHAPTER IX

WOMAN AND CHILD LABOR

EARLY ORIGIN

While women and children have always assisted in the work of the home, it was not until the development of the factory system that they began to work for wages outside of the family. From the earliest days the preparation of food, spinning and weaving and making up of garments, and other branches of domestic economy had been the peculiar tasks of the housewife. With the removal of the textile industries from the home to the factory and the invention of light-running machinery, many women followed them and employment was found also for young children. Thus with the inception of the modern factory system and machine production there arose the problem of woman and child labor. In England the evils of the early factory system were incredibly bad. Professor Walker wrote: [1]

The beginning of the present century found children of five, and even of three years of age, in England, working in factories and brickyards; women working underground in mines, harnessed with mules to carts, drawing heavy loads; found the hours of labor whatever the avarice of individual mill owners might exact, were it thirteen, or fourteen, or fifteen; found no guards about machinery to protect life and limb; found the air of the factory fouler than language can describe, even could human ears bear to hear the story.

[1] *Political Economy*, p. 381.

117

Conditions were never so bad in this country as in England, owing to the later development of the system and prompter legislation against its evils, and especially to the scarcity of labor which compelled employers to make the conditions of labor more attractive.

THE FIELD OF EMPLOYMENT

The field of employment for women has been a constantly expanding one. When Miss Harriet Martineau visited the United States in 1840 she found only seven occupations generally followed by women: teaching, needlework, keeping boarders, work in the cotton mills, typesetting, bookbinding, and domestic service. Since that time the area has widened until there is scarcely an occupation in which women are not found except those closed to her by law or by physical inability. The number of females 10 years of age and over engaged in gainful occupations was 2,647,000 in 1880, or 14.7 per cent of the total female population; this number more than trebled in the next thirty years, being 8,075,772 in 1910, or 23.4 per cent of all.

The largest number employed was in domestic and personal service, and next to that in manufacturing and mechanical pursuits, though even in that branch they were most numerous in the traditional branches of woman's work, as dressmakers, seamstresses, etc. It is nevertheless in the manufacturing industries that the most serious evils connected with woman and child labor are found. The problems differ greatly in different sections of the United States. In the Atlantic states the greatest proportion of women as compared with men find employment and give rise to special problems of women's work; in the South child labor is more conspicuous, while in the West both woman and child labor are of relatively small importance.

EFFECT OF WOMAN LABOR UPON THE OCCUPATIONS OF MEN

An interesting question suggests itself at this point: Is the increase in the employment of women at the expense of men? Are the women crowding the men out of their occupations and taking their places? At first inspection the statistics of occupations would seem to lead to an affirmative answer, for the percentage of women breadwinners increased from 13.5 per cent in 1880 to 17.6 per cent in 1910, while that of the men fell from 80 to 76.8 per cent, and that of the children remained about the same. The cause of the change in the proportion of the sexes was not due, however, to any falling off in the number of men, but to the great influx of women into the ranks of wage-workers. In some lines of employment, like those of bookkeepers, stenographers, typewriters, clerks, etc., there has undoubtedly been an encroachment and men have been displaced. But on the other hand many occupations have been opened to men during the last fifty years that were unknown before, such as the expanding fields of railroad construction and operation, the steel industry, the utilization of electricity, and other similar lines. In most of these the muscular effort involved or the character of the work has kept women out, but in other lines where special rapidity or lightness of touch are required the women outnumber the men, as in the manufacture of cotton goods, hosiery, hats and caps, etc.

The development and improvement of machinery has of course favored the employment of women. Mr. John A. Hobson [2] asserts that "in modern machinery a larger and larger amount of inventive skill is engaged in ad-

---

[2] *Evolution of Modern Capitalism*, p. 297.

justing machine-tending to the physical and mental capacity of women and children.'' He concludes that if the exploitation of these forms of cheap labor had not been prevented by factory legislation and by public disapproval, ''the great mass of the textile factories of this country [England] would have been almost entirely worked by women and children.'' As a matter of fact one of the reasons for the great expansion of woman labor in the United States as well as in England is because it has been found cheaper than man's labor. We are thus brought face to face with a fundamental question in the discussion of the problem: Why are women paid lower wages than men?

WAGES OF WOMEN

As to the fact there is no doubt; one comparison taken from the census of 1900 will be sufficient to illustrate it. The annual average earnings of men in mechanical and manufacturing industries were $490 and of women $272 per annum. The more important question is why this difference exists. A number of reasons suggest themselves at once. In the first place women are less efficient than men and produce less; hence they are paid less. In some industries, particularly those requiring physical strength, women cannot compete successfully, and those are usually the highest paid employments. Other well-paid industries are regarded by men as essentially their own and social pressure is applied to keep women out. Then, too, woman's ambition to attain industrial efficiency is not so great, owing to her expectation of marriage and release from industrial life. Women are more often absent from work, owing to sickness and domestic claims upon their time; this irregularity of employment tends to reduce their efficiency. But even in employments

where the efficiency of men and women is admittedly
equal, the women receive lower wages in the majority of
cases. According to a report of the Bureau of Labor, in
80 out of 100 cases where the women did the same work
as the men and did it as well, they received lower wages
than the men. This leads to the consideration of a second
group of causes, which have to do with woman's standard
of living.

One reason why she receives less is because she is able
and willing to live on less. Physiologically, Dr. Atwater
has said that man needs one-fifth more nutriment than
woman. Women's wages are less because of their somewhat lower cost of subsistence. But even aside from this
fact, the frequent partial dependence of women upon
other members of their family for support makes them
willing to accept less and consequently reduces their
wages. The average American workingwoman is young,
only about twenty-two and a half years old, and after the
age of twenty-five is reached the number declines rapidly.
That is to say, working girls regard their employment
as a temporary affair, remaining only about five years, on
the average, in the store or factory; during this time they
often live at home with their parents and are content to
receive a wage much smaller than a man would require
as head of a household.

The third reason is, however, the most important, because it explains at the same time the low economic position which woman occupies in the industrial world. The
narrowing of the field within which women can readily
find employment has the effect of greatly intensifying
the competition within that field. There is also a great
reserve army of potential women wage-earners, whom a
slight increase of wages or force of circumstances—loss
of employment by the male members of the family—will

bring into the field as competitors. There is, in other words, a constant over-supply of labor in most women's industries, which does not exist in any men's industries except the most unskilled.

Women exhibit, furthermore, a comparative lack of mobility from one industry to another, as well as from one locality to another. According to Professor Smart, women are so unready to leave home that their pay on one side of narrow Scotland is 50 per cent lower than that on the other side.

In the same way, the flow of labor from one occupation to another, which tends to equalize the advantages and rates of pay of different employments, is far feebler among women than among men.

Finally, there is little organization among women. Their individualistic, almost jealous, attitude to one another prevents their combination and united action, while their submissive acceptance of what is offered leads to apathy. They have only infrequently formed unions and endeavored to substitute collective bargaining for individual action. Women are therefore industrially in much the same situation as unskilled, unorganized male laborers, and the remedy in both cases would seem to be the same—education and organization.

The Effects of Woman Labor

The presence of a large supply of cheap woman labor undoubtedly has a depressing effect upon men's wages, and consequently upon the standard of life of the whole laboring class. George Gunton [3] is authority for the statement that "in proportion as the wife and children contribute to the support of the family the wages of the

---

[3] *Wealth and Progress*, p. 171.

father are reduced.'' The family wage tends to remain the same whether it is earned by the father alone or by the father with the assistance of his wife and children. It is, however, not quite clear in most cases whether the men's wages are low because the women and children work, or whether the women and children work because the men's wages are low. It may fairly be concluded, however, that the evil effects of low wages for women are not confined to themselves but are felt by all with whom they come in competition.

READJUSTMENT OF WOMAN'S WORK

What conclusion shall we draw, then, in view of all these facts, as to the desirability of employing of women? The fact of their low wages and industrial dependence is not sufficient to lead one to condemn it. These are transitional phenomena and can be remedied. Women have always worked—on the farm, in the home, and in making household supplies. When this work was taken over by the factory, woman became a wage-worker in the modern sense.

The census records in respect to the labor of women, therefore, read in the light of collateral facts, are a history of industrial readjustment rather than a record of the relative extent of the employment of women, and it is impossible to say, so far as the census figures are concerned, whether a larger proportion of women are actively engaged in labor today than formerly or not. The one fact which is clear is that factory or shop work is displacing home work, and that this readjustment of industrial conditions is leading to the employment of women outside the home in constantly increasing numbers.[4]

[4] Report of Industrial Commission, Vol. XIX, p. 926.

The effect of this readjustment has been to increase greatly the production of wealth. The production of household supplies was removed from the family to the factory when it was handed over to machinery and done better and more cheaply. If the work of women thus released were expended for no useful purpose, society would gain only in the increased leisure of the women. But if these then took up other new lines or set men free from old employments so that they could turn to still different ones, then the production of goods could be greatly increased. Mr. George L. Bolen [5] writes on this point as follows:

Without women's help their work in stores and offices would be done by men taken from other employment. The latter's present work would have to be stopped to that extent, lessening the quantity of goods produced by men. The effect would be the same as if a farmer had to stop plowing two hours before noon to go to the house and cook his dinner. * * * Women behind the counter, and at the typewriter, release men for work that women cannot do.

From the standpoint of woman herself, industrial independence must be regarded as a great gain. Set free from the necessity of contracting marriage for the sake of a home and of depending upon mere sex attraction to attain that end, she will develop her capacities more fully and when she does enter upon marriage will do so as a result of mutual attraction. The entrance of women into gainful occupations must be regarded as an essential step in their own progress and the improvement of society.

CHILD LABOR

Quite different must be our attitude towards child labor, which can only be condemned as a waste of labor

[5] *Getting a Living*, p. 475.

power and as stunting the development of the children. The census of 1870 stated for the first time the number of children at work in the United States; there were 739,164 between the ages of 10 and 15 years, of whom 114,628 were employed in manufactures. During the next decade the number increased over 58 per cent to 1,118,356 children at work in all occupations. The disclosure of such an undesirable tendency called forth restrictive legislation in most of the states and the number declined materially by 1890. Since 1890 however there has been a reversal of this tendency back to the conditions of 1880, owing chiefly to the industrial development of the South, where almost no factory legislation exists as yet. In 1910 there were 1,990,225 children at work between the ages of 10 and 15 years, or almost one-fifth of all the children of those ages.

In the South Atlantic states the proportion of children at work is especially high, reaching 58 per cent of the boys and 45 per cent of the girls between 10 and 15 years of age in South Carolina.

EVILS OF CHILD LABOR

The evils connected with child labor are the long hours —usually 11 or 12 hours a day where no restrictive legislation exists—and the exhausting and often dangerous work. The effect of monotonous and exhausting toil on the health of the children before their muscles are set and their frames knit is thoroughly bad; they are stunted and deformed and prematurely aged. Many of the occupations, too, in which child laborers are most numerous are dangerous or injurious, as, for example, tin can factories, saw mills, paper box factories, type foundries, and tobacco establishments. Second only to the physical effects of child labor is the mental and moral injury suffered not merely by the child but also by society in depriving these youthful laborers of a thorough education. While it is well that children should be kept busy, there is no compensating reward either in money wage or preparation for adult life in such monotonous, profitless drudgery.

The influence of the competition of children upon wages is depressing, and their employment indicates either a willingness on the part of employers and parents to exploit this cheap and defenseless form of labor, or a backward state of civilization. Such an evil can be cured only by determined public opposition, by the passage of laws forbidding all labor by children under a certain age, say 15 (except possibly in agricultural work or housework), compelling school attendance, and providing for careful inspection. Most of all is needed an aroused public conscience.

LABOR LEGISLATION

Labor legislation is the most effective method of improving the conditions of employment, and to a consideration of this subject we must devote the remainder of this section. We have already seen that the fundamental principle of our modern wage system is freedom of contract. This is guaranteed in our federal and state constitutions as both a personal and a property right. As a result of this fact the courts have generally declared unconstitutional any legislation, designed to protect the interests of labor, that seemed to abrogate this freedom of contract or that savored of class legislation. Efforts to improve the condition of labor by legislation have therefore met with especial obstacles in this country. On the whole, however, means have been discovered of evading these constitutional restrictions when it has seemed clearly demanded by the welfare of society, and the history of labor legislation in this country is one of fairly steady progress. The early laws were practically confined to imprisonment for debt, mechanics' liens, the hours of education of children employed in factories, and similar matters. Nothing noteworthy was accomplished until 1866, when Massachusetts passed an eight-hour child labor law for children under fourteen; in 1874 she passed a ten-hour law for women and children under eighteen engaged in manufacturing establishments, and in 1877 enacted the first factory inspection act, an idea which has since been copied in most of the states and without which mere legislation is of little avail.

FACTORY ACTS

The factory acts may be divided into two classes: (1) those that endeavor to secure the safe or healthful manner of conducting a business and (2) those that attempt to limit the occupations, the hours, and the methods of paying the workers. Under the first head come such matters as fire protection, ventilation, guarding of machinery, inspection of boilers and mines, etc. Such legislation and inspection have in many states been extended to churches, school-houses, hotels, theaters, and public buildings.

The second group includes those laws which are usually meant when factory acts are referred to. In England there has been a very steady development and extension of such legislation, beginning in 1802, when Peel's Act tried to limit the hours and time of work of pauper apprentices in the cotton mills; this was extended to all young people in textile industries in 1833, to women in 1844, then to all large industries in 1864, and to smaller ones in 1867, and finally in 1878 these various provisions were codified into a complete factory act regulating the health and safety of the laboring people generally.

In the United States the movement was considerably later and has not been so uninterrupted. But today laws limiting the number of hours of labor to eight for all those engaged on public works have been passed by the federal government and by most of the states. Attempts to fix the hours of labor of adult male workers have usually been declared unconstitutional, for the reasons stated above, except in especially dangerous or unhealthful establishments, such as bakeries, mines, smelters, and similar lines. Consequently the men have been forced to rely largely upon their own efforts for the redress of industrial grievances; in this fact lies one explanation of the growth and strength of labor organizations in this country.

On the other hand legislation in behalf of women and especially children—wards of the state—has usually been held constitutional by the courts and has had a more extended application. More than half of the states of the Union have regulated the length of the working day for women and children. The tendency now is to limit the working day for women to eight hours, and that of children to even less. Child labor laws limit the age below which employment is illegal, usually between 10 and 14 years, but even as high as 16 years. Within these ages employment may be allowed only in exceptional cases by means of an employment certificate or permit. A few states require a physical and mental examination of the child before the permit will be issued. There is a tendency to require compulsory schooling of some kind until the age of 16, either in the regular schools or in continuation schools. All this labor legislation in behalf of women and children is based upon the biological and ethical principles of the conservation of human resources and the perfection of the race.

Along with all other legislation in behalf of labor, there is a tendency to regulate the periods of rest for working people, both for their own welfare and the safety of society. In railroad work and in other work, a maximum period of continuous employment is prescribed and a certain period of rest is required between work periods to allow the workmen to recuperate. This movement is still further emphasized by the organized efforts for one day of rest in seven. Modern industrial organization does not permit the faithful observance of the Sabbath as a day when all regular toil shall cease. The one-day-of-rest-in-seven laws are designed to give every workman at least one day of rest in each week, letting that day come at such a time as industrial or personal convenience will permit.

MINIMUM WAGE LEGISLATION

One of the most recent tendencies of labor legislation is the movement in behalf of minimum wage laws for women and children. The example for such a law, which was set by Massachusetts in 1911, has been followed by other states and bids fair to become general. These laws vary somewhat in character. Usually they provide for a central state board which has charge of the enforcement of the law. This board, either alone or with the assistance of a local board made up of representatives of employers, employes, and the public, determines upon a fair minimum wage in each of the industries of a locality. Some of the boards have merely advisory powers and depend upon mediation, publicity, and public opinion to carry out the findings of the commission, while others have compulsory administrative powers to carry out their or-.

ders, with the aid of the courts if necessary. In at least one case, a fixed minimum wage has been prescribed in the statute. The tendency, however, seems to be to provide a board with large discretionary administrative powers.

These minimum wage laws are based upon the principle that an industrial worker is entitled to a fair living wage. The justice of such a claim cannot be gainsaid. The question of what shall be done with those incapable of earning the minimum wage, either because of deficiencies in training or physical disabilities, is a serious one. It can probably be solved by allowing exceptions to the law and wise administrative discretion in its enforcement. In general we may conclude that by the passage of such legislation, society has definitely decided that there are some conditions of employment which cannot safely be left to free contract or to collective bargaining between employer and employe, but must be regulated by society itself on the broad grounds of social welfare.

TEST QUESTIONS

1. What were some of the early origins of woman and child labor?

2. What evils were connected with the early factory system in England?

3. Are the women crowding the men out of their occupations and taking their places?

4. What are the most important reasons for woman's low wages in modern industry?

5. How does Mr. Bolen justify the employment of women?

6. What are the chief evils of child labor?

7. Into what two classes may the factory acts be divided?

8. Why has the movement for enlightened labor legislation been slower in the United States than in most European countries?

9. What are some of the most common features of child labor legislation?

10. What are the essential characteristics of the minimum wage legislation for women?

11. What evidence may be cited in proof of the contention that the modern woman labor problem is chiefly a matter of the readjustment of woman's work?

12. What biological and social questions are involved in woman labor?

13. Why have the courts been more liberal in the construction of laws regulating the labor of women and children than in the interpretation of the laws regulating the labor of men?

14. What is the significance of the one-day-of-rest-in-seven movement?

CHAPTER X

EXTENT OF UNEMPLOYMENT

The greatest problem in modern industry, as well as the greatest curse to the laboring classes, is unemployment. While unemployment has always existed under all systems of labor, it assumed added significance when the introduction of the wage system threw every worker upon his own resources and made him responsible for the care of himself and his family. Modern industry is sensitive and unstable, and its delicate mechanism is very likely to get out of order; credit and fashion, to mention no others, are factors that make for instability, and these are essentially modern. Professor Marshall is of the opinion that the factory system has not increased inconstancy of employment, but has simply rendered it plainer by localizing it. But whether more or fewer than in earlier times, the number of the unemployed in modern industry is appallingly great.

It is not easy to estimate correctly the extent and amount of this evil and we accordingly find considerable variations in the statistical presentations of fact. In 1885 two investigations of the amount of employment were made, one by Carroll D. Wright, in his report as United States Commissioner of Labor for 1886, and the other by the Massachusetts Bureau of Labor in its report for 1887. Mr. Wright defined the unemployed very narrowly as ''those who under prosperous times would be fully employed, and who, during the time mentioned, were seeking employment''; using the term in this restricted sense, he concluded that 7½ per cent of the working population engaged in manufacturing and mechanical pursuits and trade and transportation were idle during the year, which moreover he considered one of extreme depression. The Massachusetts statistics, on the other hand, were presented as indicative of general conditions in normal years and may safely be regarded as such. According to this report, 30 per cent of the total number of breadwinners in the state had been unemployed at their principal occupations on an average of 4.11 months in the year covered; some of these, however, found work at other or secondary occupations. But the net result of the investigation was well put in the terse statement of the report that ''about one-third of the total persons engaged in remunerative labor were unemployed at their principal occupation for about one-third of the working time.'' At the lowest estimate the whole working population lost on the average almost one-tenth of their working time. The loss of such a proportion of the community's productive force, with all the demoralization attendant upon irregular or no labor, is evidence of a problem of grave import.

CLASSIFICATION OF THE UNEMPLOYED

Unemployment is such a broad term and covers so many different ideas that it will be well to classify the unemployed before proceeding further. They may be logically divided as follows:

I.   The temporarily unemployed
    a. Those certain of work again (efficient workmen temporarily out of work, owing to seasonal variations, shut-downs, etc.)
    b. Those without such a prospect
        1. Efficient and industrious workmen thrown out of work by change in fashion, introduction of new machinery, foreign competition, prolonged depression, etc.
        2. Those whose work is naturally fluctuating and casual in its nature (casual day-laborers, charwomen, etc.)
II. The permanently unemployed
    a. The "won't works" (like tramps)
    b. The "can't works" (defectives in general)

Such a classification renders much easier the analysis both of the causes and of the cure of unemployment.

Causes of Unemployment

The first question that presents itself in any discussion of the causes of unemployment is whether it is due primarily to personal causes, such as inefficiency or intemperance, or to industrial causes over which the individual has no control.

Personal causes are those mental, moral, and physical defects which show themselves either in the inability and inefficiency of the workman or in his unwillingness to work. Here are included all the varieties of personal inaptitude, ranging from idiocy, intemperance, and vice, to old age, sickness, and accident.[1]

Such a comprehensive definition includes many cases, of course, where no blame can be attached to the individual, and yet each one of these causes is personal, that

---

[1] Report of Industrial Commission, Vol. XIX, p. 746.

is, it does not affect at the same time a whole group, as an industrial depression would do. Persons included in this group are always on the margin of employment; in bad times they are the first to be discharged and in good times they are the last to be employed. Nor is the cause of their lack of employment always easy to give; it may be itself the result of industrial accident or unhealthful occupation, or the result of heredity, evil habits and associations, and defective education. We may present two tables giving briefly the causes of poverty and unemployment. The first gives the causes of poverty ascribed by the charity organization societies of New York, Boston, and Baltimore to applicants for relief:

CAUSES OF POVERTY

CHARITY ORGANIZATION SOCIETY RECORDS [2]

CAUSE	PER CENT	
Drink	13.7	
Shiftlessness and inefficiency	7.5	
Other moral defects	2.1	
Total, Character		23.3
No male support	5.0	
Lack of other normal support.........	3.6	
Total, Support		8.6
Lack of employment	23.5	
Insufficient employment	8.1	
Poorly paid, etc.	3.3	
Total, Employment		34.9

[2] Warner, *American Charities*, Rev. Ed., p. 53.

CAUSE	PER CENT	
Sickness and death in family..........	21.1	
Insanity and physical defects.........	4.1	
Old age..............................	3.9	
Other incapacity	4.1	
Total, Incapacity		33.2
	100.	100.

The first group of causes indicates misconduct and the last group indicates misfortune; the other two shade off into industrial causes, though lack of employment—the largest single cause—may in turn be ascribed to any one of several remoter causes according to the bias of the investigator. This table is a record of the causes of failure on the part of those who have fallen behind or dropped out altogether in the race of life. At the other end of the scale stand the members of labor organizations, on the whole, the elite of the labor world. The following table gives the causes of unemployment of 31,339 cases at the end of September, 1900, as reported to the New York Bureau of Labor Statistics:

CAUSES OF IDLENESS, MEMBERS OF TRADE UNIONS, 1900

CAUSE	PER CENT
No work	75.5
Bad weather	.5
Strike or lockout........................	13.0
Sickness	4.7
Superannuation	1.6
Other causes	4.7
Total	100.0

This table emphasizes very strongly the industrial causes of unemployment, three-fourths of which is ascribed to lack of work. In some cases, as among the iron and steel workers, where there is a regular two months' shut-down to make repairs, and in the building trades, where the inclemency of the weather usually prevents work during the winter, the lack of employment may be regarded as a vacation rather than a hardship, for the rates of pay are high enough during the remaining months to offset those of idleness. In other cases, however, as in coal-mining, there is a large reserve army of workers on hand and employment is secured from only one-half to two-thirds the time. In 1900, when the average number of days of employment was larger than it had been in ten years, the bituminous miners were employed only 234 days and the anthracite miners only 166 days in the year. This indicates a very bad organization of the industry. The same thing was formerly true of the London dockyards, where there was a reserve army of some 4,000 surplus workers. Of course the effect of this is to depress wages. The clothing trade is subject to seasonal fluctuations and the caprice of fashion, wherefore it offers very irregular employment.

Machinery and improved processes were frequently spoken of by witnesses before the Industrial Commission as the leading cause of unemployment. If the general conditions of business are good at the time of the first introduction of machinery, the displaced laborer is reabsorbed again and the hardship is not so noticeable. But if it coincides with a period of business depression, the introduction of machinery appears to be the cause of a large displacement of labor, which might more truly be ascribed to industrial depression. This last cause is responsible for enormous suffering among the laboring classes, for the method oftenest resorted to by industrial enterprises to reduce expenses is the wholesale discharge of laborers, who are thus made to bear the burden of industrial disorganization. This was well illustrated by the economies effected by the railroads in the year 1908, in their general reduction of the labor force and of wages.

But even in good years the inconstancy of employment is startling. In the four years 1897-1900 the men in trade unions in New York State lost 16.2 per cent of their time from unemployment, which is almost exactly one day in every week. And these, it must be remembered, were skilled and efficient workers in organized trades. Finally strikes are given as a cause of unemployment in the table; these are a peculiar feature of modern industry and do not call for further discussion, except to point out that they are not so important as they are often represented to be.

Remedies for Unemployment

The foregoing analysis of the causes of unemployment shows that they are deep-seated in the nature of modern industry and that it would be unjust to the workingman to attribute them in any large measure to his incapacity or indisposition to labor. The care of the unemployable must of course be undertaken by society in order that such persons may be prevented as far as possible from depressing the wages of competent labor by their competition. Exceptional periods of distress may and should be met by temporary relief measures. But what we may call the normal unemployment in modern industry, which amounts to from 2 to 2½ per cent of the labor force, cannot be overcome by direct methods. The remedy for this lies ''in a better organization of employers and employes, more steady expansion of trade, and greater stability of industry and of legislation affecting industry. These are not directly problems of unemployment, but rather of taxation, currency, monopoly, immigration, overproduction, and technical advances in industry. Their treatment must be undertaken, not primarily as measures of providing for the unemployed, but as measures for improving the conditions of business." [3]

The problem of unemployment would thus seem to be a permanent one, bound up in the very nature of a dynamic society; it may be regarded as the price of progress. But the question may fairly be raised as to whether the laboring classes should foot the bill or whether the cost might not fairly be borne by society as a whole. This has suggested, as a solution of the problem, insurance of workingmen against unemployment, a discussion of which, however, must be deferred to the end of the section. Some methods of alleviation, if not of abolition, of the evils of unemployment may be suggested. Free public employment bureaus and agencies, national in scope and well integrated, would do much to secure a better adjustment of demand and supply in the labor market, and secure a better distribution of the labor force and greater mobility of labor. To prevent the loss through strikes and lockouts, better organization and mutual understanding on the part of both employers and employes is needed. And finally, improved industrial and technical education is essential, whereby the loss in skill through the introduction of new inventions and machinery may be minimized and the productivity of the laboring class increased.

Among the measures of relief for unemployment due to accident, sickness, and old age, none is more important

[3] Report of Industrial Commission, Vol. XIX, p. 757.

or more deserving of a hearing in the United States than that of insurance against these evils. The earnings of the average male wage-earner are so small—half of the number earn annually less than $436, and half of the adult male factory workers earn less than $400 a year—that the unemployment, sickness, disablement, or old age of the breadwinner must throw a large proportion of families so afflicted into a condition of periodic poverty. Any remedies that will alleviate the miseries caused by fluctuations in employment, industrial accidents, diseases incident to industry, etc., deserve a respectful hearing.

INDUSTRIAL ACCIDENTS

No adequate statistics of industrial accidents exist in the United States, but a recent estimate by F. L. Hoffman[4] gave the number of fatal accidents among occupied males in 1908 as between 30,000 and 35,000. An analysis of the reports of the New York Bureau of Labor Statistics from 1901 to 1906 shows that of the total number (39,244) of industrial accidents reported in that state a little over 2 per cent were fatal, almost 17 per cent resulted in permanent disablement, and 81 per cent resulted in temporary disablement. More than half of the accidents in industry are the result of machinery in motion. Mr. Hoffman calculates that "it should not be impossible to save at least one-third or perhaps one-half by intelligent and rational methods of factory inspection, legislation, and control." Prevention of accidents rather than compensation to the workingman after they occur should be the aim of society, in order to avoid the wasteful loss of productive power, not to mention the suffering and misery entailed by such accidents. "Immunity, not com-

[4] Bulletin of United States Bureau of Labor, Sept., 1908, p. 418.

pensation," has been the demand of the British trade unions. Of first importance then is careful factory legislation, safeguarding of machinery, and factory inspection.

Marked advances have been made along these lines as a result of governmental regulations and greater co-operation among factory inspectors, employers, and employes, and as a result accident rates have been very much reduced during the last few years. A strong educational campaign has been carried on by state labor bureaus and various local and national societies as well as by employers themselves for the purpose of acquainting all concerned with the possibilities of safety devices until "safety first" has become a popular byword. In order to make even greater systematic advances along this line, the liability insurance companies in 1913 established an Accident Prevention Bureau for the purpose of studying scientifically the possibilities of accident prevention and making this information available for all concerned. As a result of these appeals, based on considerations of humanity and economy, great strides have been made for the prevention of industrial accidents. Industry regards more the sacredness of human life, recognizes the waste in crippling or killing its trained workmen, and feels the heavy burden of accident insurance and liability awards.

Legally and judicially we have been interested primarily in the question of responsibility and compensation. Until recently legislatures and the courts have taken the position that the workingman was responsible unless he could prove the employer responsible for his injury. The impossibility of such proof and consequently the untenability of such a position are clear from the following table, compiled by the German Government for purposes of accident insurance:

ACCIDENTS IN GERMAN INDUSTRIES TRACEABLE TO DIFFERENT CAUSES

CAUSES	AGRICULTURE (1891)	INDUSTRY (1887)	MINING (1887)
Fault of employer	18.2	19.8	1.3
Fault of injured workman	24.4	25.6	29.8
Fault of both	20.1	4.4	...
Fault of third person	2.8	3.3	4.3
Unavoidable or indeterminable.	34.5	46.9	64.6
Total	100.0	100.0	100.0

CAUSES OF ACCIDENTS

Statistics from both Germany and Austria show that a full half or more of all industrial accidents are due to causes for which neither employers, injured workmen, nor fellow employes are responsible, but which are incidental to the nature of the industry itself. But besides the danger of injury from machinery, there are numerous specially dangerous or injurious trades in which injury by poisoning, disease, etc., is almost unavoidable as trade processes are at present conducted. These have been classified as follows: trades in which lead is a poisonous element, trades which produce other chemical poisons, trades in which lockjaw is an incident, trades in which the danger arises from injurious particles in the air or from dust, processes that require a sudden change from heat to cold and vice versa, those that require artificial humidity, and trades in which accidents are so frequent as to demand special legislation. Before we try to decide who in justice should bear the cost of sickness or injury arising from these causes, let us inquire as to the practice in the United States and in other countries, so as to have the data necessary for a fair conclusion.

EMPLOYERS' LIABILITY

The original legal doctrine regarding liability for accident in England and America, which until recently was practically unmodified in the latter country, was based on the principle of individual responsibility for acts of negligence. Briefly stated the common-law doctrine is that an employer must provide reasonably safe conditions of employment and that then the employe assumes the risks incident to the occupation or arising from the carelessness of fellow-servants; moreover even if the employer has been remiss, the employe cannot collect damages if he has been guilty of contributory negligence. These three doctrines—assumption of risk, doctrine of the fellow-servant, and contributory negligence—have been used practically to free the employer from all responsibility in cases where injured employes have sought to secure damages. Moreover, as has been shown above, many cases exist where it is impossible to fix the blame on either employer, employe, or a third party, and in such cases no compensation could be secured for injury under the law. The full rigor of the common law, which has worked out so unfairly for the workingman in modern machine production, has been modified in most of the states by statutes defining more exactly the duties of the employer and repealing the fellow-servant doctrine in certain lines of employment, notably in railroad work.

WORKMEN'S COMPENSATION

Under the common-law doctrine, compensation for industrial accidents had to be sought by injured workmen through a suit for damages against the employer. Recovery was very uncertain for the workman and what he did recover was largely consumed in legal expenses. In 1906 and again in 1908 Congress passed a federal employer's liability act limited to common carriers, which was still based upon the principle of negligence; that is, it proceeds upon the assumption that somebody is to blame for every accident that occurs.

A number of states have recently enacted workmen's compensation acts, which are based upon the principle that accidents are as much factors in the cost of production and distribution as labor or material, and that therefore the consumer ought to bear the charge. Under these laws the injured workman or those dependent upon him are entitled to a regular schedule of pay for accidents. Indemnities may be paid either by the employer carrying his own risks, by indemnity insurance companies in which the premiums are usually paid by the employers, by employers' mutual companies, or from a state fund to which each industry contributes in proportion to its schedule as an accident risk. In some states the compensation system is compulsory. In others it is voluntary. In the latter case the employer is usually deprived of the common-law defenses if he chooses not to accept the provisions of the law. Some state laws provide that the employes shall contribute a small amount to the insurance fund.

Germany was the first country to introduce the principle of compulsory accident insurance in 1884. Employers are there organized into associations and sections and are compelled to bear the expense of granting compensation to injured workingmen, which compensation amounts to about two-thirds of their average wages. In 1897 England, by the passage of the Workmen's Compensation Act, adopted the principle "that a workman is entitled for all accidents of occupation to a moderate and reasonable compensation.'' Practically all the advanced industrial nations of the world have passed laws to compensate sufferers for all accidents in industry, thus placing the burden of industrial accidents upon the industry as such and not upon the laborer.`

Sickness, Old-Age, and Unemployment Insurance

As we have seen, sickness and old age are still more usual causes of poverty and unemployment than accident. All the arguments for compulsory insurance therefore apply with peculiar force to these evils. Germany was again the pioneer in the establishment of these forms of insurance. In 1883 sickness insurance was organized, being made compulsory for all persons with incomes under $500; one-third the expense is borne by the workers and two-thirds by employers, the main purpose being to secure a sufficient relief—amounting to one-half the wage —for a period of thirteen weeks. In 1889 invalidity and old-age insurance was introduced for the same class; contributions are made in equal proportion by employe and employer, the state contributing about $12 a year to each annuity. Pensions are granted after thirty years of payment or to those over seventy.

In 1908 Great Britain passed a still more comprehensive measure, providing for a pension for all citizens of seventy years or over who have been residents for twenty years, in accordance with a sliding scale based upon private income, the pensions ranging from five shillings weekly down to one shilling. Finally, insurance against unemployment was tried in Switzerland in 1893 to 1897, but was finally abolished, owing to abuses and difficulty of administration. The question, however, continues to be a live one for discussion and legislative proposals.

Old-Age Pensions in the United States

Old-age pension systems have made their beginnings in the United States through various private and public schemes. Many cities have established pension systems for their public school teachers, policemen, and firemen. There is a widespread agitation in favor of pensioning all civil service employes of the cities, states, and nation. Logically this movement cannot stop short of including all industrial toilers who are in need of such support.

Already a number of private concerns have established elaborate pension systems for the benefit of their employes. The great railroad systems were among the first to make these provisions and today old-age pensions are found on most of the roads. In the steel business Andrew Carnegie had set aside a fund of $4,000,000 for the benefit of the employes in his works. Later the United States Steel Corporation dedicated $8,000,000 for this purpose and consolidated the two in the United States and Carnegie Pension Funds. The International Harvester Company has a very comprehensive old-age and disablement pension system. The Western Union Telegraph Company on January 1, 1913, set aside $1,000,000 for this purpose. Butler Brothers' Wholesale Houses have long had such a plan in operation, and many similar systems are to be found in other industries. Mention should be made of the Carnegie pension system for superannuated college and university teachers.

These old-age pension systems which have been established by private concerns are not receiving general approval and especially not from the most immediate beneficiaries, the laborers. The great objection to them is that the workmen do not receive these benefits of right. These corporations cannot afford to provide these benefits as a system of charity distribution. They must receive some financial return for their outlay in the form of steadier and more faithful employment as well as greater loyalty from their workmen. The pension relief plans are usually beset with conditions which limit the freedom of the laborer in his efforts for self-improvement. The pension system often acts as a system of intimidation, in that workmen must not ask for higher wages, shorter hours, better working conditions, or even participate in labor union activities, of which some of these firms disapprove, under penalty of arbitrary discharge from service, even after long years of employment, and loss of their pension privileges. For these reasons private pension schemes cannot satisfy the strong social demand for old-age benefits.

There are probably no more important practical economic problems than those connected with unemployment and workingmen's insurance. Slowly the conviction has spread that under present conditions of industry workingmen cannot fairly be held responsible for industrial accidents, and that with prevailing wages they cannot be expected to save enough to maintain themselves in sickness and old age. It therefore becomes the duty of society so to organize industry and legislation that the terrors of accidents, sickness, and old age shall be reduced to a minimum.

TEST QUESTIONS

1. How does Carroll D. Wright define unemployment?
2. According to Professor Marshall, what has been the effect of the factory system upon unemployment?
3. How may the unemployed be classified?
4. What are the chief causes of unemployment?

5. How can the modern employer help to reduce unemploy ment among laborers?

6. What are some of the economic changes necessary to reduce unemployment?

7. Is there any educational problem connected with unemployment?

8. According to statistics, what are the chief causes of industrial accidents?

9. What is meant by the doctrine of assumption of risk?

10. What is meant by the doctrine of the fellow-servant?

11. What is meant by the doctrine of contributory negligence?

12. Why are these three doctrines in their old common-law form unjust to labor in modern business?

13. How has the movement toward workmen's compensation legislation remedied these evils?

14. To what extent are sickness, old age, and unemployment cared for in Germany? In England? In the United States?

CHAPTER XI

MACHINERY AND INDUSTRIAL EFFICIENCY

EVILS OF MACHINERY

So far in the discussion of modern capitalistic production and of the various labor problems to which it has given rise we have not treated in detail the question of machinery and its effects on labor. We cannot, however, leave this subject without taking up this phase of it with considerable care. The advantages of machinery have been more often emphasized than the evils; so we may profitably begin with the darker side of the picture. President Hadley [1] enumerates three evils which are charged against machinery as now managed and operated:

1. That it displaces a large amount of human labor, thus taking income away from employes and giving it to employers. 2. That when it does not actually drive human labor out of use, it employs it in circumstances unfavorable to efficiency, health, and morals. 3. That under the best conditions it deprives the workman of independence, making him a specialized machine instead of a broad-minded man.

We cannot do better than take up these points one by one.

DISPLACEMENT OF LABOR BY MACHINERY

In answer to the first charge President Hadley flatly denies that machinery has displaced labor, but insists that

[1] *Economics*, p. 337.

"there has been a most conspicuous increase of employment in those lines where improvements in machinery have been greatest," giving the expansion of railroads as an illustration. But it is not possible to generalize from this case without further analysis. The immediate effect of improved machinery, especially if suddenly introduced, is practically always to throw men out of employment. The extent to which this will occur depends on the suddenness and extensiveness of the change, but fortunately, as Professor Nicholson points out, new inventions seldom come suddenly or are introduced all at once on an extensive scale. It took almost a generation, for example, for American machine methods to displace Swiss hand labor in the making of watches. But when such a change does occur it hits hardest the least efficient and older men, those just on the margin of employment, for a man past middle life can rarely learn a new trade.

The effect of displacement in causing suffering will also depend somewhat (1) upon the mobility of labor, (2) upon the knowledge of new opportunities and the capital to make possible a change of location or industry, and (3) upon improvements in the means of transportation. It can easily be shown that as a general principle the lump-of-labor theory—namely, that there is just so much work to be done and that if machinery is introduced for this purpose there will be less work for men to do, is erroneous. But there is this element of truth in it, that the question whether or not men will be reabsorbed in the same industry depends upon whether or not the market for the goods produced by the new machine can be expanded. If the demand is elastic, that is, can be largely extended because of the fall in price brought about by the cheaper production, as in the case of cotton goods, then the displaced laborers will probably be re-employed to produce an enlarged supply. If, however, the demand is inelastic, that is, will not be expanded by reason of a fall in price, as in the case of salt or coffins, then the displaced labor will not be reabsorbed in the same industry but must look elsewhere for employment.

Is New Employment Created?

The elaborate investigation of the Department of Labor in 1898 regarding the relative merits of hand and machine labor shows clearly the effect on the displacement of labor by the introduction of machinery. A few cases will serve as illustrations.

Hand and Machine Methods Compared

Year of Production	Articles Produced	Different Operations Performed	Different Workmen Employed	Time Worked		Labor Cost
				Hours	Minutes	
1829-30	Wheat (hand)	8	4	61	5	$3.55
1895-96	Wheat (machine)	5	6	3	19	.66
1859	Boots (hand)	83	2	1436	40	408.50
1895	Boots (machine)	122	113	154	5	35.40
1850	Carpet (hand)	15	18	4047	30	20.24
1895	Carpet (machine)	41	81	509	1	.29
1891	Loading ore (hand).......	1	1	200	0	40.00
1896	Loading ore (machine)....	3	10	2	51	.55

These cases, chosen at random, all show an increase in the number of different men employed and an immense saving in time and in labor cost. Nothing is indicated however as to the total amount of employment. Optimistic writers like Carroll D. Wright claim that if machinery has displaced labor in one direction it has created more employment for them in others.   He shows for instance [2] that in 1830 the per capita consumption of cotton in this country was 5.9 pounds, while in 1890 it was 19 pounds, and gives similar figures for iron and steel and railroad traffic.   It will be noticed that all of his examples are chosen from industries in which the demand is elastic.

Mr. J. A. Hobson, a more careful and conservative writer, draws less optimistic conclusions from a study of Great Britain.   He says:

First, so far as the aggregate of manufactures is concerned, the net result of the increased use of machinery has not been to offer an increased demand for labor in those industries commensurate with the growth of the working population.   Second, an increased proportion of the manufacturing population is employed either in those branches of the large industries where machinery is least used, or in the smaller manufactures which are either subsidiary to the large industries, or are engaged in providing miscellaneous comforts and luxuries.[3]

It must be said, however, in modification of Mr. Hobson's inferences, that it may be accounted as a social gain if the demand for manufactured commodities can be met by the labor of a smaller proportion of the population, since the energies of the rest are then set free for professional or artistic or similar pursuits.   A study of the census reports of Great Britain seems to show that this is what has happened in that country.

[2] *Industrial Evolution of the United States*, chap. 28.
[3] *Evolution of Modern Capitalism*, p. 229.

IRREGULARITY OF EMPLOYMENT

The amount of labor is not the only factor to be considered; the regularity of employment, as we saw in the last section, is of hardly less importance. Professor Nicholson says: [4]

Another danger of an entirely opposite kind lurks in this immense power of machinery, which is continually showing its reality and remedies for which will, it is to be feared, be the fruit of long years of tentative adaptation to the new environment. What all sensible workingmen desire, what the advocates of the trade unions say is their chief object, is to get a "steady sufficient wage," but it has been proved inductively that great fluctuations in price occur in those commodities which require for their production a large proportion of fixed capital. These fluctuations in price are accompanied by corresponding fluctuations in wages and irregularity of employment. But fluctuations in wages and discontinuities in employment are two of the greatest evils which can befall the laboring classes.

We have already seen how modern capitalistic methods of production may lead to overproduction and to a crisis. We now see how machine methods may cause unemployment or irregular employment. The men displaced directly by new machinery, those thrown out of work by industrial depression resulting from overproduction in machine industries, and finally those irregularly employed in the new occupations supplying luxuries—all of these may fairly attribute their suffering in large measure to machine methods.

LOWERING OF THE GRADE OF LABOR

The second great charge made against the factory system is that it displaces a higher grade of labor by a lower grade; some-

[4] *The Effects of Machinery on Wages*, p. 65.

times substituting the work of women and children for that of men; sometimes substituting work under conditions physically or morally unhealthful, for work under healthful conditions; sometimes substituting specialized and mechanical work for diversified occupation which contributes to general intelligence.

The point as to the labor of women and children has already been discussed. The charge that factory labor is physically unhealthful may in general be denied. Mr. Wright, in an elaborate defense of the factory system in the Tenth Census, concluded that the conditions of work in the modern factory are much more conducive to good health than those under the preceding domestic system, while morally they are far superior. The qualities demanded by the machine production of the modern factory are punctuality, steadiness, reliability, and sobriety, and it therefore makes against intemperance and immorality. So far as these exist in factory towns, they are the result of town life rather than of manufacturing. It must, however, be said that while the factory system is not inherently unhealthful, the high pressure at which operatives of steam-driven machinery are compelled to work, particularly in this country, may and often does wear them out prematurely. This again is partially offset by a shortening of the hours of labor.

MONOTONY OF WORK

The final charge against the factory system is monotony of work. Many writers, from Adam Smith down, take the view that it is more stupefying to make a small part of an article, say the sixty-fourth part of a shoe, than to make the whole article. Professor Marshall, who has considered the subject carefully,[5] concludes that while

---

[5] *Principles of Economics*, Vol. I, p. 315.

it takes away manual skill, it substitutes higher or more intellectual forms of skill. ''The more delicate the machine's power the greater is the judgment and carefulness which is called for from those who see after it.'' But after all there is less danger from monotony of work than from monotony of life, and the cure for this would seem to be in an increase of machinery rather than in its abolition.

Conclusions as to Machinery

Let us now try to summarize our conclusions on this intricate question. The first effect of the introduction of labor-saving machinery is to displace particular laborers; these suffer real injury, though they are often reabsorbed in the industrial organism. The social gain is undoubted, for the 'improved methods lead to lower prices and thus to an increase in the real wages of labor. To the improvement and wider use of machinery we must indeed look for the ultimate relief of the human race from exhausting toil. Says a socialist writer:

On mechanical slavery, on the slavery of the machine, the future of the world depends. * * * All unintellectual labor, all monotonous, dull labor, all labor that deals with dreadful things, and involves unpleasant conditions, must be done by machinery. Machinery must work for us in coal mines, and do all sanitary services, and be the stoker of steamers, and clean the streets, and run messages on wet days, and do anything that is tedious or distressing.

If labor today has a complaint to make against the use of machinery, it is that labor has not shared sufficiently in the improvements thus far effected. But the evil here is connected with the inequitable distribution of wealth, not with the methods of its production. In justice labor should share in the technical improvements which characterized the nineteenth century and which will revolutionize to a still greater extent the industries of the twentieth.   The practical question in this connection is as to the best method for labor to secure its claim to a share in the increased production.   One answer, to which we shall turn next, is by increasing its efficiency through better industrial education and training.

INDUSTRIAL EDUCATION

The subject of industrial education has recently been receiving considerable attention in the United States and the needs and shortcomings of our country in this regard have been described.   Under modern methods of production, with their extreme specialization of labor and extended use of machinery, it is practically impossible for a worker to secure an adequate knowledge of a trade in the actual practice of it.   In former days boys acquired training in their trades by the system of apprenticeship under the immediate charge of a master of the craft. The system of apprenticeship has today almost disappeared; boys are taken into shops as helpers, not as apprentices, and receive practically no systematic instruction in their trade, especially in a large modern establishment.   In consequence of these facts it is insisted that school instruction should be given to make good the absence of shop practice; that a general system of industrial education should be developed to give our workingmen systematic training in the various trades.   The superiority of the opportunities for industrial education on the continent of Europe, especially in Germany, has been frequently emphasized, and Germany's industrial advance has been credited in large measure to this fact. We can probably not approach the subject better than by explaining the systems in these other countries and then comparing them with that of the United States.

Beginning with Germany as the country in which industrial education has received the greatest attention, we find there three different kinds of schools, which we may call the lower, middle, and higher. The lower group includes artisan and specialized trade schools, and is intended to be a substitute for the apprenticeship system. While they have an important influence on the general industrial efficiency of the nation, they concern chiefly the small handicrafts. The middle group comprises the trade schools (Gewerbeschulen), of which the most famous are the weaving and dyeing schools at Chemnitz; other branches taught are soap-boiling, milling, building, pottery, etc. These are the schools which provide technical instruction for the large manufacturing industries, and are consequently of great importance; they train the foremen, superintendents, managers, and heads of establishments rather than the workingmen. The higher group is formed of the technical high schools or technological institutes, where the scientific experts are trained. The importance of the German system lies in the development of the last two groups rather than in provision for the training of the workmen. Germany's recent industrial advance must be credited to the training of the officers, not the rank and file, in the industrial army, to the development of managerial ability rather than of manual skill. The splendid systems of continuation schools, which have been established in many cities, are however endeavoring to raise the general standard of intelligence and efficiency of the rank and file as well as to prepare them for definite trade positions.

INDUSTRIAL EDUCATION IN ENGLAND

In England the last twenty years have seen a marvelous development in industrial education, brought about in part by the "made in Germany" agitation. The English system of industrial education differs from the German. It attempts to educate working-class boys, while at work in the mill or at the forge, to be foremen, managers, etc., mainly by means of evening classes in trade or technical schools. The German system, on the other hand, trains men who already have a superior general education. These schools are regarded as stepping-stones for the more ambitious and intelligent young workingmen. They give a practical grasp of the subjects, but do not teach actual processes of manufacture, owing to trade union objections. They thus come between the lower and middle schools in Germany. The higher technical schools also exist and have recently been greatly expanded.

INDUSTRIAL EDUCATION IN THE UNITED STATES

The system of industrial education in the United States may be said to resemble that of Germany more than that of England, as it supplies industries from above rather than from below, but it is in a very chaotic state as yet. The most important schools are institutes of technology and the technical departments of the universities, but these train men only for the highest positions. Along this same line, colleges and universities have established courses, departments, and schools in business administration for the purpose of training for the higher administrative and industrial positions. Provisions for the individual training of the workmen are gradually being made, notably in manufacturing centers. Thus there are a few trade schools resembling somewhat those in the middle German group, as the textile schools at Philadelphia, Lowell, and a few other cities. Lower grade schools and industrial high schools are found in nearly all large cities. Instruction in agriculture is given in a great many states in the public schools and in special agricultural schools.

A considerable beginning has therefore been made in industrial education, but it is still inadequate to supply the needs of the country. The work that is being given has not reached its highest possibilities for usefulness in that the contents of the courses are not always the best and the methods of instruction are crude. There is a great shortage of well-trained teachers as well as a want of a clear perception of purposes and ends. That there is a distinct need of and demand for instruction of this character is shown by the enormous expansion of correspondence schools, a peculiarly American institution, which endeavor to give the training afforded by the English schools to the more ambitious young artisans.

NEED OF BETTER TRAINING

So far in their industrial development the people of the United States have been immensely aided by two factors : (1) the rich natural resources of the country and (2) the high quality of the labor. But as we have already seen, the natural resources are being either rapidly exhausted or monopolized. As to the character of the second factor, we may quote from the testimony of a recent careful observer, Dr. A. Shadwell: [6]

The American method of work in the industrial sphere is distinguished by the following features : enterprise, audacity,

[6] *Industrial Efficiency*, Vol. II, p. 451.

push, restlessness, eagerness for novelty, inventiveness, emulation, and cupidity. Employers and employed have exhibited the same qualities in their degree.

But they suffer "from the national defect of want of thoroughness, which arises from the craving for short cuts." Now that American industries are entering the markets of the world in international competition, it becomes important to correct any faults that will cause us to fall behind.

The movement for better industrial education through the establishment of trade schools has met two obstacles in this country. The first is the hostility of the trade unions, which fear to see their control of the labor market disturbed by the annual turning out of hundreds or thousands of workers from the trade schools without any special sympathy with trade union methods or policies. The other difficulty lies in the satisfaction with prevailing methods, the belief that the American workman without training possesses skill superior to that of his European competitors, and a naïve national self-conceit in all things American. Now that we are for almost the first time in a hundred years measuring our industrial efficiency in foreign markets against our European competitors, we shall be compelled to take stock of all the items that make for industrial supremacy. There seems to be little doubt that when this is once fairly done, the need of a better system of industrial education will be recognized and met.

TEST QUESTIONS

1. What three evils are often charged against machinery?
2. What three factors have an influence on the suffering that is caused by displacement of labor when new machines are introduced?

3. According to the investigation of the Department of Labor, what effect does the introduction of machinery have on the displacement of labor?

4. How may machine methods cause irregularity in wages and employment?

5. Does the introduction of labor-saving machinery lower the grades of labor? Illustrate.

6. What can you say concerning the charge often made against machinery, namely, that it makes labor monotonous?

7. Show the need of a system of industrial education in the United States.

8. What is the system of industrial education which exists in England?

9. How does the German system of industrial education differ from the English?

10. What is the situation with respect to industrial education in the United States?

11. How does foreign competition compel us to pay attention to the problem of industrial education?

CHAPTER XII

PROFIT-SHARING AND CO-OPERATION

The Nature of Profit-Sharing

Among the reforms suggested for remedying some of the evils incident to the modern wage system those of profit-sharing and co-operation occupy a prominent place. The separation of the community into capitalists and laborers, classes different in conditions and ideals, constitutes a menace to the peace and progress of industrial society. The wage system, moreover, is thought by many to have broken down the former intimate relation of employer and worker, and some scheme is needed to correlate their interests again and to bind them together. To secure this result profit-sharing is advocated. As defined by the International Co-operative Congress in 1897 this is "the agreement, freely entered into, by which the employe receives a share, fixed in advance, of the profits." It is not a change from the present wage system, but simply a modification of that system, according to which the laborer receives a share in the profits in addition to his wages. The purpose is to identify the interests of the employes with those of their employer and thus give them some of the same motives for energy, care, and thrift in the conduct of the business. Three principal methods of profit-sharing may be mentioned, though the variations are manifold. The favorite method in England and the United States is the payment

162

of a cash bonus at the end of a fixed period, such as a year. A second plan, which is the rule in France, is a deferred participation by means of a savings bank deposit, provident fund, or annuity, for the purpose of providing for old age and disability. The third plan, which has recently grown in favor in this country, is the payment in shares of stock of the company.

Advantages of Profit-Sharing

The economic theory of profit-sharing is that by inducing greater care and diligence on the part of the employe he will himself create the fund from which he is paid. It is claimed by its advocates that it increases both the quantity and the quality of the product and that it promotes greater care of implements and materials, thus reducing the cost at the same time that it increases the output. The classic example of this is the case of the original profit-sharing scheme, the Maison Leclaire, in Paris: the result of the first six years' experiment was a dividend on wages of $3,753 a year, derived entirely from the increased economy and care of the workers. In some cases, however, the object of the employers is to secure immunity from strikes and other labor disturbances and a greater permanence of the labor force; participation in profits is conditioned upon the men's abstaining from joining a trade union or upon uninterrupted service. In these cases the deferred participation plan is used. The advantages claimed for the system are not merely the increase in product already spoken of and the greatest efficiency of the worker, but also the improvement in his material and moral standards and the promotion of industrial peace by lessening discontent and friction. The main basis for the system, since it is economic and not philanthropic in its nature, must of course be the increase in production brought about by its adoption.

Objections to Profit-Sharing

benefits uncertain

More weighty, however, appear the objections against profit-sharing, which seem to have had sufficient force to cause the failure of a number of ventures in this direction. In the first place the relation between the increased effort of a single workman and the success of a general business is so remote, especially in our complicated modern industry, that it is unlikely to act as a very powerful stimulus. But even if it should, the savings thus effected might be swept away by the poor business management of the employer.

It is quite possible that the workman who, in the hope of earning "bonus to labor," has done work 10 per cent in excess of the normal standard, may, even under a liberal scheme, find that, instead of receiving an addition to his normal wages of, say, 7 per cent, the bad management of his employer has reduced his bonus to so low a level that he has to be content with a supplement equivalent to only 2 per cent on his wages, or that, as has been the case in a large proportion of the schemes * * * no bonus whatever is forthcoming.[1]

It is undesirable to make the earnings of the laborer dependent in any way upon the fluctuations of business or the ability of the employer. The ordinary wage system has at least the merit that the reward of the laborer is made dependent only on his own efforts. The lot of the modern worker is too unstable and employment too

[1] Schloss, *Methods of Industrial Remuneration*, p. 305.

unsteady to add a new element of uncertainty in wages. If the laborer has really earned the premium, say labor leaders, why not add it to his wages instead of adopting this roundabout method? The sliding scale, or a system of premiums or bonus payments for increased output, would be better than profit-sharing, and is rapidly spreading.

LIMITS FREEDOM OF LABOR

This leads to the second objection, namely, that profit-sharing paralyzes the efforts of the laborers to better their own conditions through trade unions, strikes, or other methods. The trade union attitude was vigorously stated by President Gompers, of the American Federation of Labor, in his testimony before the Industrial Commission: [2]

There have been few, if any, of these concerns which have been even comparatively fair to their employes. * * * They made the work harder, longer hours, and when the employes of other concerns in the same line of trade were enjoying increased wages, shorter hours of labor, and other improvements, tending to the material progress of the worker, the employes of the concern where so-called profit-sharing was the system at the end of the year found themselves receiving lower wages for harder work than were those who were not under that beneficent system.

As long as the system is viewed with suspicion by the laborer or used as a weapon in industrial bargaining by employers, the plan is foredoomed to failure. But even were it managed in the proper spirit, it is after all applicable to only a comparatively few industries, namely,

[2] Report, Vol. VII, p. 644.

those in which labor makes up the largest part of the cost of production. In most modern industries capital plays such an important role as compared with labor that the field for this plan is comparatively limited.

FUTURE OF PROFIT-SHARING

In the actual practice of profit-sharing there have been many interesting experiments and not a few failures. It may be said to date from 1842, when M. Leclaire, a Parisian painter and house decorator, introduced it into his business. The practice has since spread over France and England; it has met with little success in the rest of Europe. In the United States the movement has been more recent and of smaller proportions. The reason for this is suggested by President Hadley as follows: [3]

Where the laborers under the old wage system are not working up to a high standard of efficiency, there is more chance for the success of profit-sharing. This seems to be the reason why it works better on the Continent than in England, and better in England than in America.

The United States Steel Corporation has adopted a system of profit-sharing which benefits only managers and those higher up in the service. This plan attempts to encourage efficiency in production by increasing the interest and efficiency of management.

The future of profit-sharing seems uncertain. A great many of the schemes which have been tried at one time or another have been abandoned. Labor will probably continue to oppose profit-sharing schemes which do not aim toward labor partnership in industry. Such a system has been adopted in the South Metropolitan Gas

[3] *Economics*, p. 377.

Company, England, where the laborers are permitted to elect three of the members of the board of directors. In this direction, as a step to a full partnership of labor in industry, there may be a greater future in profit-sharing.

Co-operation

More far-reaching than profit-sharing, which involves only a change in the method of payment of wages, is co-operation, which involves a change of management as well. Its final goal, in the minds of its advocates, is the radical modification if not ultimate abolition of the present wage system. While profit-sharing is paternalistic and is directed to an increase of production, co-operation may be said to be democratic and to aim at a more equitable distribution. Under this plan the laborers hope to divert to themselves the large amount of profits which they now see going into the possession of their employers. By eliminating the manager or enterpriser they hope to save his profits for themselves. Three different kinds of co-operation are usually distinguished: (1) distributive or consumers' co-operation, (2) producers' co-operation, and (3) financial co-operation for credit, banking, etc. We may take these up in turn.

Consumers' Co-operation in England

Successful consumers' co-operation may be said to have originated in Great Britain when twenty-eight Rochdale workingmen founded their famous society of Equitable Pioneers. The success and growth of this remarkable experiment, starting in 1844 with a capital of £28, to a system of 8,000 members, with a capital of £200,000 in 1874, is a most romantic story. It was largely imitated and retail co-operative stores sprang up all over England. It is estimated that at the present time about a third of the population of England is supplied through co-operative stores, and that these stores return annually about $60,000,000 into the pockets of the workingmen. These savings are often used to build homes, and thus the co-operators actually ''eat themselves into house and home.'' These results are in accord with the ideals of the pioneers of the movement, who were more than store-keepers and penny-savers. They were noble-spirited men who looked upon the co-operative system as a great workingmen's betterment movement.

English co-operative stores soon discovered their absolute helplessness against the wholesaler and the jobber. They were often discriminated against and always felt that these distributors constituted another group of middlemen enterprisers that ought to be eliminated. In response to these needs and feelings, the English Co-Operative Wholesale Society was organized in 1864, for the purpose of joint purchase of supplies for the retail co-operative stores. It effected large savings and was successful from the beginning. In 1911 the English Co-operative Wholesale Societies reported a business of about $250,000,000. The Scottish Wholesale Society was organized upon the same plan and has been equally successful.

From buying, the society soon passed to making its own goods and now manufactures a long list of commodities, thus establishing its economic independence and completing the industrial chain. The society already owns and operates the largest flour mills and the largest boot and shoe factories in England. These factories are owned by the co-operative society as the enterpriser. They are not conducted upon any system of co-operative production, but work just as any other capitalistic plant would.   The profits go to the co-operators as consumers, not as producers.

EXPERIMENTS IN THE UNITED STATES

In the United States experiments of this kind have in general had only a brief existence thus far. It is impossible to say how many such societies exist today, as no adequate statistics on the subject exist. Trade union stores in New England, the grange stores of the Patrons of Husbandry, and later similar ones of the Sovereigns of Industry show what has been attempted along one line. Three distinct groups of consumers' co-operative enterprises which have been more or less a success should be mentioned. They are the Zion's Co-operative Mercantile Institute, of Salt Lake City, Utah, which is both a retail and wholesale society, under the control of the Mormons; the Rochdale stores, of California, with the Rochdale Wholesale Company, of San Francisco; and stores established under the auspices of the Right Relationship League in the upper Mississippi Valley states. The reasons for the lack of success in this country are not hard to find. Co-operation requires a willingness to take considerable trouble for small economies, which American workingmen, with their generally high wages, have not yet been willing to do. It also requires a considerable degree of homogeneity in thought and interests on the part of a people, which is naturally less present in the United States with its large admixture of foreign population than in England or the countries of Europe.

METHODS OF DISTRIBUTION

The methods of the Rochdale Society will serve as an illustration of the way in which the savings effected by

co-operation are distributed among the members.   Any
one might become a member upon payment of one shilling and was then entitled to trade at the store.   The
prices charged were those current in the town, but purity
of goods was assured; cash payments were an essential
feature.   At the end of the year the profits were divided
among the members in proportion to the amount of their
purchases.   On the other hand it may be noted that no
attempt was made to introduce profit-sharing with the
employes, who are paid ordinary, but good, wages only.
In general the plans laid down by this original society
have been followed by all successful consumers' co-operative stores in whatever place or country they may be located.   This sort of consumers' co-operation has met
with considerable success in continental Europe as well.
It has been estimated that about 50,000,000 people the
world over, equal to half the population of the entire
United States, are supplied by co-operative retail stores.

Producers' Co-operation

Producers' co-operation differs from that just described in that it is a union on the part of laborers to do
away with the employer and to secure for themselves the
profits.   The object of the first is to lower prices for the
co-operators as consumers; the object of the second is
rather to secure higher prices for themselves as producers by eliminating the profits of the industrial manager.   They hope to perform his function by their collective effort and to manage as well as to labor; indeed
by diminishing friction and strikes they even hope to
increase the profits.   Examples of successful co-operation of this sort are not numerous, as it has great difficulties with which to contend.   Most of the experiments
have failed, though recently it would seem that the move-

ment is making substantial though slow progress, especially in France and England. Most of the successful ventures in the latter country, however, seem to be of simple industries, as agriculture and dairy-farming.

The most notable example of successful productive co-operation in the United States has been furnished by the coopers of Minneapolis, who organized a shop of their own in 1868 and have steadily increased their business since that time. Other instances often cited are the wood-workers in St. Louis and boot and shoe companies in Massachusetts. More recently there has been a considerable extension of co-operative creameries, cheese factories, and similar businesses of a simple kind. Producers' Co-operative Marketing Societies are common in agricultural regions. The grain-growing regions usually have their co-operative elevators and storehouses and frequently produce exchanges. The largest concern of this kind is the California Fruit Growers Exchange, with a membership of more than 6,000 producers and an annual business of more than $20,000,000.

FINANCIAL CO-OPERATION

In a system of credit co-operation, the co-operators desire to benefit themselves by the use of their combined capital and combined credit, which are used, as it were, for the common good of all. The forms of co-operative financial societies are those which undertake to supply insurance or credit, like co-operative insurance companies, co-operative banks, co-operative credit societies, and building and loan associations. Co-operative fire insurance companies and building and loan associations have been quite successful in the United States, but credit insurance has been neglected. The latter branch is receiving a great deal of attention at the present time, and we may look for progress along this line within the next few years. The economic possibilities of such credit associations are well illustrated from some of the German societies which have become strong enough to go into the national money markets for their loans. Their securities have often sold at better figures than government bonds. These savings are secured for the benefit of the individual borrowers of the society. Such societies perhaps cannot exist without special legislation in their behalf.

ADVANTAGES OF CO-OPERATION

The advantages of co-operation are summed up as follows by Professor Walker.[4] From the laborer's point of view:

First, to secure for the laboring class that large amount of wealth, which * * * goes annually in profits to the employer. Second, to secure for the laborer the opportunity to produce independently of the will of an employer. * * * In addition to these, the political economist beholds in co-operation three sources of advantage. First, co-operation would, by the very terms of the case, do away with strikes. * * * Second, the workman would be incited to greater industry and to greater carefulness in dealing with materials and with machinery. Third, in no small degree frugality would be encouraged.

To these may be added other advantages, mostly realizable, however, in consumers' co-operation. Saving in store-room, clerk hire, advertising, bookkeeping, etc., is effected, while, above all, the practice of cash payments saves all loss from bad debts. The initial success of the Rochdale pioneers was due in large part to the economy in this line, as a system of long credits burdened the re-

[4] *Political Economy*, pp. 344, 345.

tail trade of England at the time they began. In this country the large department stores have introduced this system and have thus been able to give their customers lower prices and to that extent have lessened the motive for consumers' co-operation. The educative effect of successful co-operation upon the participators in developing habits of thrift, careful management, and a knowledge of business principles, is one of the chief advantages of the system.

The ultimate ideal of enthusiastic co-operators does not, however, stop short at a mere saving in price. The goal is stated as follows by the Right Relationship League of America, which has several co-operative stores in the Northwest: Consumers' co-operation is merely the first step which "will lead next to co-operative production, next to public ownership of natural resources and finally to complete industrial and economic equality, social and political right relationship—the Kingdom of God on Earth."

DISADVANTAGES OF CO-OPERATION

The defects of co-operation have already been suggested in the account of their failure. In the first place the importance and need of intelligent and efficient management are usually underrated by workingmen. They are unwilling to pay high salaries and as a consequence lose the best men and secure inefficient service. Co-operation has therefore succeeded best in retail trade where the processes are comparatively simple, or in those branches of production where industry counts for most and management for least. But even if it were possible to secure an efficient and progressive manager for a co-operative shop, it is found very difficult for a man chosen by the workmen to enforce discipline among them. A second disadvantage is the difficulty of securing capital. Where, as in many branches of large-scale manufacturing today, the average investment of capital amounts to more than $1,000 per employe, the impossibility of obtaining this by the contributions of the workers is obvious. Nor are capitalists usually willing to lend to such organizations, as the risks are too great. To meet this difficulty Ferdinand Lassalle, a German socialist, proposed that the state should advance the necessary capital to associations of workmen. But the experience so far with productive co-operation would seem to suggest that the social benefits would not equal the waste of public capital. There is danger also that if successful the co-operative associations would tend to become monopolies; they are profit-seeking societies and would probably not differ materially in their methods from ordinary joint stock enterprises.

It seems impossible, therefore, to expect from co-operation a final solution of the labor problem, such as John Stuart Mill, for instance, hoped for. Where successful, however, it has succeeded in distributing profits among a larger number of persons than would otherwise have received them. Its educative and moral effects, too, in the appeals which it makes to higher motives and to character, are of the highest value. But as an industrial system of enterprise it cannot supplant the present system so long as the manager of industry is needed. Today he performs a useful social service and profits are his pay therefor. If he is to be eliminated, society must first be raised to a higher plane of efficiency, intelligence, and morality. But just because it makes these high demands upon the members of the laboring class, attempts at co-operation should receive all reasonable encouragement.

TEST QUESTIONS

1. What is meant by profit-sharing?
2. What is the chief purpose of profit-sharing?
3. What are the three principal methods of profit-sharing?
4. What objections are raised against profit-sharing?
5. What is the system of profit-sharing used by the United States Steel Corporation?
6. According to President Hadley, under what conditions does profit-sharing have its greatest chances?
7. How does co-operation differ from profit-sharing?
8. To what extent has consumers' co-operation developed in England?
9. How are profits distributed under the Rochdale method of consumers' co-operation?
10. To what extent does consumers' co-operation exist in the United States? Give a few prominent examples.
11. What is meant by producers' co-operation? Give a few examples. Why is producers' co-operation less successful than consumers' co-operation?
12. To what extent has financial co-operation developed in Germany? In the United States? Why are we backward?
13. What are the chief advantages and disadvantages of co-operation?
14. What is the ultimate ideal of enthusiastic co-operators?

CHAPTER XIII

MONEY AND BANKING

CREDIT ECONOMY

Probably on no subject has there been such confused thinking or have such widely varying views been held as on that of money. There is, however, substantial unanimity of opinion on the important points among economists today, though in practice there still remain many unsolved problems. The modern industrial system has already been characterized as one of capitalistic production, of large-scale enterprises with extended use of machinery. Not less fundamental are the processes of valuation and exchange made possible by the use of money and credit; and also by the machinery for the geographical distribution of goods by our railroads and steamship lines.

The modern stage of economic development has been described by Hildebrand as one of credit economy, as opposed to those of barter and money economy which preceded. It is inconceivable that the modern complex system of exchange could be maintained without the extended use of money and credit. Without attempting to define these terms or to trace their historical development, we may proceed at once to state some of the problems to which they have given rise.

176

VALUE OF MONEY

The first question that suggests itself is: What determines the value of money? The generally accepted answer may be briefly stated: The value of money depends, other things remaining the same, upon its quantity. According to the quantity theory an increase in the supply of money will cause a fall in the value of each unit, just as an increase in the supply of wheat or cotton will cause a fall in the value of each bushel or bale. Conversely, a decrease in the quantity of money will cause a rise in the value of money. It is simply an application of the general law of value to money. The phrase "other things remaining the same" is an important one, for it assumes that the amount of business and the methods by which it is conducted will remain substantially unchanged. Of course if an increase in the amount of money is accompanied by an equivalent expansion of trade, the one may offset the other and the value of money remain unchanged.

Now inasmuch as the prices of all goods and services are measured and expressed in terms of money, it is clear that a fall in the value of money means a rise of general prices; the value of each commodity is now expressed in terms of a larger number of less valuable units or dollars. Prices will be high if the quantity of money in circulation in a country is large; they will be low if the quantity is small. Which is better for a country, high prices or low prices? To this question it may be answered that it is a matter of indifference, provided only that there is enough money to do the work of exchange efficiently and that fluctuations are prevented. Just how much constitutes enough is, however, a matter of contention. In the undeveloped sections of our country, where capital is scarce and banking facilities undeveloped and where most of the people are debtors, there has always been a demand for cheap and abundant money. Capital and money have been confused and the need of one has led to a demand for the other.

Rising and Falling Prices

It is not a matter of indifference, however, whether prices are rising or falling, that is, whether inflation or contraction of the currency is taking place. A period of falling prices means hardship and injustice to debtors and producers of goods, such as farmers, manufacturers, etc. Having contracted obligations and engaged in the production of commodities with the expectation of a given price, they find their goods worth less when ready for the market and as a result they are confronted with a loss instead of the anticipated profit. Under such circumstances a contraction of the currency and falling prices mean lessened production of wealth. Consequently many writers, and even so good an economist as President Walker, have urged that a slow steady inflation of the currency would promote trade and "give a fillip to industry." The monetary history of the United States is filled with attempts to realize this in practice. Colonial and revolutionary bills of credit were first issued; when these were forbidden by the new Constitution resort was had to issues by state banks. When the federal government began the issue of greenbacks and restricted the use of state bank notes, the inflationists looked to this source for assistance. After the defeat of the Greenback party, they turned finally to the coinage of silver, which was now falling in price, and the question of bimetallism in the United States was made a practical political issue.

BIMETALLISM

Down to 1870 practically all the nations of Europe and America had the system of bimetallism at ratios of 15½ or 16 to 1. About that date the great increase in the supply of gold and the fall in the value of silver led one country after another to abandon the latter and to adopt the system of gold monometallism. This was vigorously resisted by many persons and several fruitless efforts were made to secure a system of international bimetallism. Failing in that, the friends of silver in this country endeavored to secure independent action by the United States alone, and were ultimately successful in obtaining the purchase by the federal government, for coinage purposes, of practically the entire silver output of the country during the years 1878-1893.

The arguments in favor of bimetallism are as various as the motives of its advocates, but two or three of the more important ones may be briefly stated. It is urged because it would give a more stable measure of value than either silver or gold alone could do; and the evil effects of fluctuations in the value of gold since 1873 are pointed out to illustrate this contention. Monometallists answer this by asserting that most of the price changes can be accounted for by improvements in production; that even if they were caused by a contraction of the currency, this was simply one of the risks of business; and finally that the evil effects of falling prices are offset by a corresponding reduction in interest rates.

A second argument of the bimetallists was the alleged insufficiency of gold on which to do the world's business. As this has been practically met by the phenomenal increase in gold production in the last decade, especially since the gold discoveries in Alaska, it is not necessary to dwell upon this argument. On January 2, 1915, the per capita circulation of money in the United States reached $35.50, the highest point in our history. A final argument of the bimetallists concerns foreign trade. Bimetallism would facilitate this by establishing a fixed par-of-exchange between all countries. While the weight of this may be admitted, it has been practically deprived of all force because of the adoption of the gold standard by virtually all the industrially developed nations of the world. This last fact shows that the question has now been actually settled by the logic of events and today the issue of bimetallism has only an academic interest.

GOVERNMENT PAPER MONEY

Another problem connected with money which has been removed from the arena of oratory to that of calm discussion is that of government paper money. It is urged, with much truth, that if a nation issued paper money instead of gold or silver, it would save all the expense of mining these metals. It would resemble, as Adam Smith said, the discovery of wagon roads through the air in the realm of transportation.

Another argument advanced in favor of government paper money is that it would be possible by a scientific adjustment of the issues to regulate the amount of money in circulation and so to prevent all fluctuations in prices. Both contraction and inflation would be prevented and a cheap and yet ideal system of money would exist. Still others see in this form of money an instrument for the creation of wealth; this last argument simply results from a confusion of ideas and need not be dealt with.

A sufficient answer to the other two is an appeal to the lesson of history. No government which has embarked upon the issue of paper money has ever been able to restrict the issues within reasonable limits; often it has led to national bankruptcy and the repudiation of the entire issues. The experience of the United States with the greenbacks has been more fortunate than that of many countries, but does not tempt to further experiment.

KINDS OF MONEY IN THE UNITED STATES

The monetary situation in the United States today may be regarded as fairly well settled. Although we have a very heterogeneous assortment of different kinds of money, a fairly distinct sphere is allotted to each, and as the basis for all, the gold standard has been definitely established by law. Money of large denominations consists of gold and gold certificates (lowest denomination, $10), of Federal Reserve notes, of greenbacks and national bank notes (lowest denomination, $10, though one-third of bank notes may be $5); the needs of retail trade are met by the issue of silver certificates and silver dollars, and of fractional currency. The system would be much simplified by the retirement and destruction of the $346,000,000 in greenbacks, but as there is now 50 per cent reserve in gold back of them, little danger need be apprehended from their presence. Many people have regarded the existence of some $500,000,000 worth of silver dollars as a menace to the goodness of our money supply, but as the amount of gold in circulation increases, the silver will form a constantly smaller percentage of the whole. It is a cumbersome and not very valuable asset of the nation, but is now almost powerless for good or ill.

THE FUNCTION OF CREDIT

Important as is the subject of money and essential as is the need of a standard of undoubted goodness, it is overshadowed in practical significance by the problems of banking and credit. An investigation by the Comptroller of the Currency some years ago showed that over 90 per cent of the receipts of the national banks consisted of credit instruments, while probably 60 per cent of the trade of the country was carried on by credit rather than by cash transactions. A credit transaction is a transfer of goods or money for a future equivalent; the element of time is introduced. This makes possible an enormous increase in the number of exchanges and obviates the necessity, to a large extent, of using money. Most of us enjoy personal credit, which is limited only by our ability to persuade other people to trust in us. But this power of purchasing things without immediate payment must be made readily available if the ordinary business man is to make use of it. This is done through the medium of a bank, whose business it is to discount the notes of its customers, which in turn is based upon confidence in their prospective earnings. The bank credit thus obtained may be transferred by means of checks to other persons and to other banks. It is the most fluid and volatile means of payment yet devised, and is subject to dangers and abuses. In the last analysis business based upon such a system of credit rests upon confidence in the honesty of individuals and in the enforcement of the law governing contracts, and also in the ability of those who have pledged themselves to future payment to make good their obligations. In times of panic credit fails and resort is had to money.

BANKS

The fundamental institution in our credit economy is the bank, and it is therefore essential that it be thoroughly safe and responsive to the needs of the business world. A bank may furnish its customers with the ready means of payment they need in exchange for their future promises either in the form of bank notes or bank credit. The former are more largely used on the continent of Europe and in rural districts in this country, the latter by England and the United States, especially in the cities. The preference for one or the other seems to be a matter of geography.

ELASTICITY OF CURRENCY

The issue of bank notes, which was confined to the national banks, has always been very carefully safeguarded since the establishment of the national banking system in 1863. Under this system every national bank, upon its organization, was compelled to buy government bonds and was then permitted to issue bank notes up to the par value of these bonds. These notes were consequently absolutely safe, but they lacked one essential quality of good bank money in that they were quite inelastic. That is to say, the amount of bank notes did not vary according to the needs of business, increasing to meet an increased demand, as at crop-moving time, and then declining again when the demand had passed; but being based upon government bonds, they varied with the amount of the nation's indebtedness, and even then only very slowly. There was no immediate connection between the volume of bank notes and of business needs.

The main practical problem connected with our banking system therefore seemed to be the finding of some other basis for the issue of bank notes. Various plans were suggested, as the establishment of a central bank with sole power of issue, like the government banks in European countries or the Canadian system of branch banking, but Congress could not agree upon a measure.

In 1908 however a step forward was taken by permitting national banks to issue additional notes upon deposit of approved bonds and securities other than government bonds. This gave some elasticity to the system but was avowedly only a compromise measure and will expire on June 30, 1915. Finally by act of December 23, 1913, an entirely new system of banking was introduced under the name of the Federal Reserve System. It went into effect on November 16, 1914. The main features of the new system are set forth in the following paragraphs.

THE FEDERAL RESERVE SYSTEM

The country is divided into twelve regions in the principal cities of which regional reserve banks are to be established. These regional reserve banks are aptly designated "bankers' banks." Their capital will be supplied for the most part by the member banks, which are all the national banks in each district, and such state and other banks as may care to join the system. These reserve banks will do business only with the member banks, performing various services for them, which marks a new departure in our banking practice. One of these is rediscounting notes and acceptances held by the member banks which are based upon commercial transactions, import and export business, and to a limited extent upon real estate. Another is the keeping of fixed percentages of the legal cash reserves of the member banks. Under the old national banking system these reserves tended to be concentrated in New York City and in that city in about twenty banks. This massing of reserves stimulated stock exchange speculation, as much of it was loaned to speculators on call, and made it difficult for the country banks to recall their reserves in time of panic or special need. Under the new system the cash reserves of the 7,500 national banks are distributed in twelve regional reserve banks scattered widely over the whole country.

ASSET CURRENCY

The most important change introduced is the creation of an asset currency instead of a bond-secured currency. Federal Reserve notes are to be issued to member banks, secured by an equal amount of commercial paper accepted for rediscount. The volume of such notes outstanding will consequently vary with the amount of bank loans, that is, with the needs of business. Against these notes the banks must keep a 40 per cent reserve in gold for purposes of redemption. Provision is also made for the gradual retirement of the old bond-secured national bank notes. Finally, strict governmental control is provided for through the establishment of a Federal Reserve Board, made up of the Secretary of the Treasury, the Comptroller of the Currency, and five others to be appointed by the President.

SAVINGS BANKS

So far we have been discussing commercial banks, but there is another kind of institution which goes by the same name but serves quite a different purpose, namely, the savings bank. The essential and almost the only requirement of such an institution is safety. As we have seen, it is not only desirable, for personal reasons, to inculcate habits of saving and thrift in individuals, but it is also necessary to secure the accumulation of capital needed in modern industry. It is therefore important that such institutions should be widespread, accessible, and thoroughly trusted. These requirements are well fulfilled by postal savings banks now in operation in all the leading countries. Such banks accept very small savings accounts, and often do not carry any large single items. But due to the fact that they possess the confidence of the people and appeal to millions of small savers, they have led to a great increase in savings and deposits wherever they have been established. On September 12, 1914, the deposits in the postal savings banks amounted to about $28,000,000.

TEST QUESTIONS

1. What is meant by the establishment of modern business on a credit basis?

2. What determines the value of money?

3. What is the effect of an increased supply of money on the prices of commodities? Of a decreased supply of money?

4. Why does a new community usually clamor for cheap money, while an old and established community prefers a scarcity of money?

5. What effect does a period of falling prices have upon debtors? Why?

6. Why did the agricultural people of the western states strongly favor bimetallism during the years 1890-1896?

7. Would it be possible for our government to resort entirely to a paper money basis? Why?

8. What are the chief kinds of money now used in the United States?

9. What are the principal functions of a bank in our present system of credit economy?

10. What is meant by elasticity of the currency? How may it be secured?

11. What is meant by asset currency?

12. Explain the currency system established under the Federal Reserve plan.

CHAPTER XIV

TRANSPORTATION AND COMMUNICATION

MONOPOLISTIC NATURE OF TRANSPORTATION SERVICE

Almost as important for the conduct of modern industry as machine methods and credit are the rapid means of transportation and communication furnished by our railroad, steamship, express, post-office, telegraph, and telephone systems. Indeed the development of industry on a national scale and its integration under centralized control have been made possible only by these improvements.

But not only have these businesses rendered the centralization of industry possible; they themselves exhibit, on a national scale, concentration of control. They are all industries of increasing returns and lend themselves naturally to monopolistic control. At the very beginning of railroad construction one of the most far-sighted managers enunciated the doctrine that "where combination is possible competition is impossible." For years competition was regarded as the regulator of rates, pooling between railroads was forbidden, and canals were advocated as competitors. By every possible device it was sought to stimulate competition. We are at last beginning to recognize the monopoly character of the railroad industry and to regulate it accordingly.

RAILROAD CONSOLIDATION

Consolidation in the railroad world is not a new phenomenon nor is it confined to that industry, but it has proceeded further there than in any other line of business. The first form which combination took was that of pooling, according to which the traffic was pooled and the earnings then divided among the companies entering into the pool according to some previous agreement. This was forbidden by the Interstate Commerce Act in 1887 and even more stringently by the Anti-Trust Act of 1890, and accordingly railroad managers next resorted to actual consolidation of competing lines. Where this has not been possible or desirable, virtual combination has been secured by the so-called "community of interests" arrangements, based on the acquisition by one road of enough stock in competing lines to secure representation on their boards of directors.

Today some five or six groups of capitalists control over two-thirds of the railway mileage of the United States. The late Mr. E. H. Harriman was credited with controlling, directly or indirectly, a system aggregating over 67,000 miles. These great consolidations have followed mainly the territorial groupings of railroads; the United States has now been districted out by a few large transportation companies, much as France, Italy, England, and other European countries had previously been divided up. Consolidation has in many instances resulted in increased convenience to the public and in economies in management and operation, but it places a dangerous amount of power in the hands of a few men, which has not infrequently been abused and should clearly be under strict government control.

RAILROAD RATES

.The primary economic problem connected with railways is always the question of rates. This has been called in a recent book "the heart of the railroad problem." The first fact that strikes the student of the subject is the great reduction in rates and fares in the past twenty-five years, especially in freight rates. From 1.24 cents in 1882 the average revenue per ton mile received by railroads in the United States has decreased to .733 cents in 1914. Freight rates, especially through rates for bulky traffic, are considerably lower in this country and passenger fares are somewhat higher than those in effect in Europe.

But the vital problem connected with rates is not as to their relative cheapness or extortionateness; it concerns rather the granting of discriminating rates. Discriminations may be of three kinds: (1) those between different classes of goods, (2) those between localities, and (3) those between persons.

The first group is based upon the classification of freight and rests upon differences in cost of shipment, in bulk, in risk, etc. If reasonably employed, this kind of discrimination is justifiable. Local discriminations, that is, charging different rates to different localities for substantially the same service, are not only unwarranted in most cases, but are shortsighted as well. Where superior facilities or especially keen competition exists, lower rates may be permitted for favored localities, but the arbitrary exercise of such powers by railway officials is thoroughly unjustifiable. Even less defensible is the practice, now happily less frequent, of granting discriminatory rates to favored individuals or corporations. They have been given by means of secret rates and rebates, by under-billing and under-classification, by free passes, etc. Both of these latter evils have been forbidden or greatly restricted by the passage of the Interstate Commerce Act in 1887 and by subsequent legislation.

GOVERNMENTAL REGULATION OF RAILROADS

The public nature of railroads is now fairly well recognized in our law and is beginning to be understood by the people at large. Railroads enjoy peculiar privileges in the grant of corporate franchises and charters, in the right of eminent domain, and in enormous grants of land and money which have been made to them in this country. Moreover, the social character of their duties is emphasized in the functions they perform, and they are under the necessity of maintaining a constant service open to all. Though they are owned by private investors and managed as private enterprises, they are essentially public enterprises as to their privileges, functions, and duties. Consequently most of the states have now undertaken, through commissions, to regulate the railroads in the public interest. These state commissions differ in power. Some have mandatory powers, that is, powers to prescribe and enforce maximum rates, while others have only supervisory powers of investigation and report. Some act only upon complaint, while others act both upon complaint and upon their own initiative. In many states this power has been given to a state public utility commission, which has control over all public utilities within the state.

While the state commissions have done and are doing valuable service, it is clear that the growth of giant railroad combinations which traverse several states necessitates federal control. The appointment of the Interstate Commerce Commission in 1887 established the principle of federal regulation, which has been slowly extended, until today the commission has extensive powers over railroads, including the control of rates.

PUBLIC OWNERSHIP

Owing to the individualistic character of our institutions and law, public ownership of railroads does not exist in the United States, which thus forms, together with England, almost the sole important exception to the world's practice in this regard. On the continent of Europe government ownership is the rule. Public control through either ownership or regulation by commission is essential in order to secure an equitable adjustment of public and private rights and to prevent the abuse of monopoly power inherent in the very nature of railroads. Public ownership has many advantages and has given satisfactory results in Europe. But for the United States the principle of private ownership with stricter governmental regulation has been definitely laid down; the problem of the future is simply how far that control shall go.

OTHER TRANSPORTATION AGENCIES

The discussion of our steam railroads does not exhaust the subject of transportation. A recent and important development is the growth of electric interurban railways, which are opening up districts untouched by the more expensive steam roads and exercising a marked influence in rural districts upon business and social life.

A more significant problem, both because of its close relations to the railroads and its monopoly character, is offered by the express companies. Organized at a time when railroads were new and undeveloped, they took over the safe and expeditious delivery of small and valuable articles. They have since grown in importance and power; three large companies now control most of the business. Since they are generally in the form of partnerships and not of corporations it has not been possible to bring them under legal control, and their rates are extremely high—three or four times as much as freight rates. In some cases the railroads, in order to gain the profits from these high rates, have organized express companies to operate over their lines. Even where that is not done, the express companies are performing a service which could as well be performed by the railroads themselves and at lower rates.

These facts, as well as the successful examples of parcel post systems in England and Europe, finally led the government to establish a parcel post system in this country in 1911. From the very beginning it proved a success, and the scope of its usefulness has gradually increased. The parcel post system at once necessitated the adjustment and lowering of express rates and caused the express business of the country to fall off appreciably.

Telephone and Telegraph

The importance of the telephone and telegraph in our modern industrial life cannot be overestimated. As means of transmitting intelligence they have served to bring the most distant parts of the world into almost instant touch and have made possible the modern centralization of business. Both offer the same problems of monopoly that we have seen exist in other parts of this field, the telegraph business being completely monopolized by two large companies, the telephone business by one, all strongly entrenched behind patents. The desirability of public ownership of these utilities rests upon stronger grounds than in the case of railroads and is strongly urged by many conservative writers.

WATER TRANSPORTATION

Although attention has usually been centered upon the railroads in any discussion of the transportation question in the United States, there are important practical problems connected with both the inland and the ocean water transportation. The questions of constructing artificial inland waterways and of subsidizing our foreign merchant marine are vital political and industrial issues. The United States is probably better provided with internal navigable natural waterways than any other country. Its navigable rivers comprise some 18,000 miles, affording access to the very heart of the continent both from the Atlantic coast and from the Gulf. They form a cheap and convenient means of transportation, especially for bulky and cheap articles; 30,000,000 tons a year are carried on the streams of the Mississippi Valley alone, though much of the former traffic has been diverted to the railroads. On the northern border of the country the Great Lakes form an unrivaled series of inland seas. The traffic on these lakes shows a great increase every year, amounting now to over 60,000,000 tons annually. The federal government has performed useful service in improving the conditions of navigation along these natural waterways, and it is now considering a comprehensive scheme for their further improvement.

CANALS

A very different problem is offered by our canal system. During the period 1820-1840 many canals were constructed by the states to connect existing waterways and to provide an outlet for produce from the interior. The best examples of these were the Erie and the Ohio canals. After the development of the railway, however, traffic began to be steadily and then rapidly diverted from the canals to these quicker avenues of transportation. Many of the canals were bought up by their rivals and permitted to fall into disuse, while those retained by the state governments remained mere shallow ditches, unimproved and ill-adapted to modern needs. The construction of the Panama Canal by the federal government and the recent expenditure by the people of New York State of over $100,000,000 for the improvement of the Erie Canal have brought the question of the rehabilitation of our neglected canal system to the front again. It seems wasteful not to connect the separate links in the magnificent system of natural waterways already provided by nature, and this will probably be the next step taken. And indeed a beginning has already been made by the construction of the Hennepin Canal, the Des Plaines Canal, and the Cape Cod Canal.

It must however be borne in mind that there are two distinct types of canal: (1) those which are simply short connecting links between navigable waterways and which permit the passage of vessels used on those waters; and (2) those canals which are shallow, have extensive lockage, and permit the use of only small boats, thus necessitating the transshipment of freight. One might well advocate the construction and enlargement of the first type, and yet hesitate to approve of the second. As yet, however, owing in part to the opposition and clamor of railroad interests, the question of canals has not received the attention it deserves in the United States.

The American Merchant Marine

The ocean merchant marine comprises two widely different branches, the coastwise and the foreign trade. The former is open only to vessels flying the American flag, and has shown a very steady growth; five-sixths of our ocean merchant marine today is engaged in this branch of commerce. Coal, lumber, cotton, and similar bulky commodities constitute the chief items entering into the coastwise trade. The tonnage of American vessels engaged in the foreign trade, on the other hand, has shown a steady decline ever since the outbreak of the Civil War. Foreign vessels today carry fully 90 per cent of the foreign commerce of the United States. The causes of this decline are economic rather than political, for American legislation has on the whole been very liberal to the shipping interests.

At the time the western part of our country began to be opened up and its great resources exploited, our merchant marine was one of the best in the world. But now the other opportunities for the investment of capital were so profitable and alluring, and the need of it so great, that all the available labor and capital of the American people began to be devoted to the development of their internal resources. A nation cannot do everything with equal advantage at the same time any more than an individual can. Accordingly we began to withdraw our capital from shipping and to devote it to agriculture, mining, manufacturing, transportation, and similar more profitable enterprises. Foreigners could build vessels and run them more cheaply than we could and it paid us to hire them to do it. Lately, however, and especially since the recent awakening of a national consciousness after the Spanish-American War, the patriotism of many individuals has been hurt by the thought that we had to depend upon foreign vessels for the carriage of our foreign commerce, while in the minds of others a comprehensive naval program demanded the building up of a native merchant marine.

Two questions suggest themselves here: Do we wish to stimulate this growth artificially? And, if we do, what means shall we adopt? On the second point the Merchant Marine Commission of 1904 recommended for the United States a general bounty on all shipping, such as France has, and the subvention of certain lines of steamers over ten specified routes, following the example of Great Britain, Germany, and Japan. Without committing ourselves on this point, it may be suggested that on political, geographical, and economic grounds we may expect in the near future to see the natural development of an American merchant marine. The recent removal of registry restrictions may be expected to encourage its up-building.

With the growth of our foreign trade, the accumulation of capital at home, and the building up of a strong navy, the conditions for American shipbuilding and shipping will become steadily more favorable, and we may expect to see American enterprise engage in this as in other lines of industry. Eventually we are destined to become a maritime nation.

TEST QUESTIONS

1. Explain why transportation service is of a monopolistic character.

2. To what extent has railroad consolidation progressed in this country? What are the main systems?

3. What are the three chief kinds of discrimination?

4. What are the main problems involved in the regulation of transportation companies?

5. What developments and changes have taken place in the express business during the past few years?

6. What can you say concerning the possibilities of internal waterways for the United States?

7. Show why the causes for the decline in tonnage of American vessels are economic rather than political.

8. What recent changes in the shipping policy of the United States Government are tending to build up a merchant marine?

9. What has been the history of express companies in the development of American transportation?

10. What effect has the parcel-post system had upon the distribution of goods from place to place?

11. What two distinct types of canals are to be distinguished?

12. Summarize the chief transportation problems confronting the people of the United States.

CHAPTER XV

PROBLEMS OF DISTRIBUTION

NATURE OF THE PROBLEM

So far we have discussed for the most part those economic problems that center round the production of wealth, such as the use of natural resources, large-scale production, trusts and monopolies, labor organizations, unemployment, industrial education, and co-operation. Now we shall consider briefly a few of the problems which are connected with the distribution of wealth.

Professor Blackmar [1] says that the three great problems of economic society are: "First, how to create the largest amount of utilities or wealth; second, how justly to divide this amount; and third, how to make the product minister to the permanent rather than to the transient well-being of society." The first problem we have already discussed; the second forms the subject of the present chapter; and the third will be taken up in the next chapter.

Within the last century the center of interest in the practical application of economic principles has decidedly shifted from production to distribution. The earlier writers on economics, as evidenced by the mercantilists of the seventeenth and eighteenth centuries, even Adam Smith, were chiefly interested in methods of increasing

[1] *Economics*, p. 133.

a nation's wealth. With the introduction of the factory system and the opening up of vast natural resources by improvements in mining and transportation, the production of wealth has enormously increased, and now the question of the method of its distribution or division is felt to be more pressing.

KINDS OF DISTRIBUTION

Under the term "distribution" two different processes are included, which should be distinguished before going further. The first is called "functional distribution" and concerns the distribution of the product of industry or the income of society among the different factors of production. That is to say, land, labor, capital, and managerial ability have contributed in varying degrees to the production of a certain amount of current wealth, and the problem of functional distribution is to ascertain how the net product resulting from these joint efforts is divided—(1) how much goes to rent, (2) how much to wages, (3) how much to interest, and (4) how much to profits.

The second kind of distribution is the division of the wealth of society among individuals or families; this is personal distribution and raises the question of poverty and great wealth. In discussing these problems, however, we must remember that wealth production and distribution take place in modern society under conditions imposed by the social order in which we live; these were defined as competition, private property, and personal liberty. If any modifications of the processes of distribution were desired, it would undoubtedly be necessary to alter these fundamental institutions.

Importance of Distribution

John Stuart Mill held that production was governed by natural laws, which could be ascertained and stated, but that distribution was artificial and hence that it was not possible to discover constant and certain laws governing it. Beginning mainly with Mill, the ethical question has been more and more asked as to what share each factor in production ought to get, not merely what it does receive.

Hence the question is rising more and more as to what should be the basis of division, and many proposals have been made. It is proposed that laborers combine to get a larger share. Hence we have trade unions, Knights of Labor, etc. It is proposed that capitalists and landlords give a larger proportion of the produce to the laborers than they are able to secure by mere private struggle. Hence we have proposals for profit-sharing and various charities. It is proposed that laborers combine to be their own capitalists and landlords; hence we have all sorts of co-operative and communistic experiments. It is asserted that the wealthy classes have so much power in their hands that private co-operation cannot succeed in competing against them, and hence it is proposed that all the people, through government (municipal, state, and national) secure all the means of production (capital and land, so far at least as land is used for production), and operate them collectively for the equitable good of all, the people thus being their own employers, capitalists, and landlords. Hence we have municipalism, nationalism, socialism. It is claimed that capitalists and landlords have been able to secure, and are today able to maintain, their large share in distribution, only through the favoritism of the Government. Hence we have proposals for free trade, the single tax, * * * the extreme proposals of the very great minimizing of the state in individualism, or the abolition of the Government in anarchism.[2]

[2] Bliss, *Encyclopedia of Social Reform*, article ''Distribution,'' p. 501.

In view of this very imperfect list it is not too much to say that most of the economic problems that are stirring society today are connected with the distribution of wealth.

BASES FOR DISTRIBUTION

The first question that suggests itself in the discussion of functional distribution is as to whether it is actually governed by so-called natural law. It is observable that the amounts which go to rent, wages, interest, and profits are regularly quite constant. What determines this? The socialists contend that "natural distribution" is the only just method and insist that the state should regulate this just distribution; they are not clear, however, as to what this natural method is. Henry George uses the same phrase when he says: "The just distribution of wealth is manifestly a natural distribution of wealth, and this is that which gives to him who makes it and secures to him who saves it."

All such statements beg the question, for they all turn on the use of the word "natural." Many modern economists are inclined to assert that the question of distribution is not an ethical one, not a question of what ought to be but of what is. Thus Professor Fetter says:[3] "Distribution in economics is the reasoned explanation of the way in which the total product of a society is divided among its members. It is a logical question and not an ethical one." And Professor Clark writes: "There is, in short, a deep-acting natural law at work amid the confusing struggles of the labor market." It will not be possible, in the brief limits of this chapter, to take up all the theories as to the way in which this distribution is effected among the claimants to a share of

Economics, p. 360.

the product, but a few of the more important practical results may be stated. We shall take up the four different factors in turn.

RENT

The word "rent" is used with two very different meanings. In the economic sense, the word "rent" refers to the return for the use of some natural objects and agencies, especially land. In the popular sense, the word "rent" is used to designate the amount paid to an owner for the use of land, houses, stores, boats, or anything else. The distinction will become clearer by illustration. In many of our cities the ground and building values are stated separately in the valuations that are made for the purposes of taxation. Many buildings are constructed upon land that is rented for long terms. What has given land alone this value? Evidently in all of these cases the person who pays rent, in the common use of the term, for a house or an office, pays for two factors, a ground value and a building value.

If land were unlimited in quantity and of equal value for use everywhere, no such thing as economic rent could exist. A person would simply refuse to pay land rent and would get on a piece of free land to carry on his business or build his house. Land, however, is limited in quantity, and most of the free land has been taken up. This fact accounts for the constantly increasing value of land, as a result of which Henry George argued that most of the future income of society will be absorbed by the landlords.

Land can be put to various uses, but some land is more useful or is more favorably located for some purposes than other land. Therefore some land is more valuable than other land. It is evident that good wheat-growing land yields more per acre for a given application of labor than poor land does. If sufficient of the good land could be secured to grow all the wheat that is needed for consumption, none of the poorer lands would be used. · But good wheat land is scarce and therefore the wheat-grower will cultivate poorer and poorer grades of land as the demand for wheat grows, until a certain point is reached at which the land will be valueless for wheat-growing; that is, it would cost more to grow wheat on the poorest or marginal land at the existing prices and demands for wheat than the land would return.

It is the advantage which the better land enjoys over this marginal land that gives the former value, and the more advantages it possesses, the more valuable it becomes. This advantage gives rise to rent. The holder of the better land can capitalize the excess value of his land over the marginal land for whatever purposes land is used, whether it be a building site on Broadway or wheat lands in the Red River Valley. Economic rent appears as a competitive premium paid for fertility or location. It is an excess over and above the total expenses of the more fortunate producers. It forms no part of the expenses of production and does not determine prices; in fact economic rent is a result of prices. It is due to the comparatively high price which must be paid to bring out the total and necessary product through the resort to poorer lands.

Such is the nature of economic rent as one of the factors which shares in distribution. It is evident that the owners of land are the beneficiaries in all social and industrial progress that is made. The practical problem that suggests itself is: Do we want private property in land? The socialists answer "No," but the individualists insist that the best use has been and can be made of land only by reducing it to private ownership. Between these two extremes there seems to be a tendency to demand for society a part of these social gains by means of various single tax schemes and taxes on the unearned increment of land. The whole problem of land taxation is involved in this question of rent.

INTEREST

All through Biblical history, Grecian history, Roman history, and the Middle Ages, interest was a favorite object of attack by statesmen and church leaders. Moneylending was looked upon as a disgraceful occupation and interest as usury, and therefore wrong. This early attitude of society toward interest was perhaps justifiable, because money then was borrowed chiefly to pay living expenses. In this sense it was regarded, perhaps rightly, as a sign of incompetency. There were in those days practically no opportunities for the use of money as productive capital. There is a vital distinction between borrowing for a productive purpose and borrowing to pay living expenses. The latter is undoubtedly bad practice and cannot be justified except in extreme cases. But to borrow for a genuinely productive purpose, for a purpose which will bring in more than enough to pay off the principal and interest, shows business sagacity.

Interest is the price paid for the use of capital. The interest appears as the result of an act of exchange. The question may fairly be asked: What is the equivalent? Why is $1 now worth $1.06 a year hence? A great many theories have been advanced to explain the facts, but they all seem to come to the conclusion that present goods are worth more than future goods. The lapse of time from the date at which a loan is made until it is paid creates a difference in value. The holder of a dollar has his choice. He may spend it now or he may save it for future use. The present value of a dollar is worth so much more to him that if he is to defer using it for one year he will want not $1, but $1.06 at that time. Thus interest is primarily a time value.

These time-value theories explain why lenders demand interest, but do not make clear the reason why borrowers can afford to pay interest. They can do this because the capital they borrow is used for productive purposes, and with it they produce during the year not merely the equivalent of the interest paid but enough more to afford a profit to the borrower and to replace the capital fund when it is used up. Capital is usually spoken of as so much money, and is borrowed of a bank in the form of money or a credit deposit, but in actual business productive capital is embodied in the form of buildings, machinery, agricultural implements, mercantile stocks, railways, etc. By the help of these a man can produce much more than without their use, so that he can afford to pay interest for them or for the money that gives him command over them. According to this productivity theory, interest is thus credited to capital as its reward in the functional distribution of wealth.

Socialists are attacking interest because it is the outcome of private property. Their claim is that it is based upon inequality and perpetuates inequality. Part of this contention is granted by most of the modern individualists of today. They believe with John Stuart Mill that private property should exist because it is the most expedient method yet devised for encouraging thrift, but that the institution of inheritance should be changed. In response to this feeling, the inheritance taxes are being used to break up large fortunes. In this way society periodically shares in these gains of individuals and prevents the perpetuation of the social and economic inequalities which capital and interest tend to create.

PROFITS

Profits are the reward which the manager of a business receives for his services in organizing and superintending the business. This share of the social income was the last to be recognized by economists, and its rightfulness is even yet denied by the socialists. They insist that profits are really the earnings of labor which have been withheld from the laborer by the superior skill and economic strength of the capitalist manager; they are institutional robbery, the exploitation of labor. It is not possible to take up the arguments on this point, but it may be said in a word that the manager of business contributes a needed service to the work of society just as truly as the laborer does, and receives his earned reward in the form of profits.

The analogy of profits to rent made by Professor Francis A. Walker is valuable for some purposes. He believed that profits are the result of exceptional ability or exceptional opportunity, just as rent is due to fertility of the soil or location of the land. There could be no profits if all men were equally able and if enough work could be found for all. In all industries there is a no-profits class of employers. The price of production is apt to be determined by the portion of the supply which is produced at the greatest disadvantage; that is, the cost of steel will probably be determined by the cost of production in the least economically managed plant that can continue to operate to supply the demand. Such a plant makes no profits, but only expenses. All plants that manufacture more economically than this marginal plant make a profit, and thus they gain an increasing advantage over the less fortunate producers.

If this conception of profits is taken, then profits cannot in any sense come out of wages. Wages could not be higher in those plants operating on a margin, or they would be forced out of business by the increased cost of production. Since these least efficient plants set the standards of wages for the entire industry, it can hardly be claimed that profits are taken out of wages. Profits are an inevitable element in private ownership production, just as rent follows inevitably from private ownership of land. Perhaps society as a whole has the same sort of claim upon profits as upon rent. This would seem to be one of the theories upon which a graduated income tax could be justified. Such a tax is similar to the tax on the unearned increment of land.

WAGES

Wages are the reward of labor. It is often assumed that wages are lower than they should be, that the laborer in some way is deprived of a portion of what he has rightfully earned. It is worth while to inquire briefly into how the share of labor in the distribution of the social income is determined. Various theories have been developed to explain the distributive process, of which we may notice three.

IRON LAW OF WAGES THEORY

The oldest in point of time and the most pessimistic theory held that wages were fixed by competition and the growth of population at the bare subsistence minimum, a bare starvation level. If by some happy chance wages were raised above this point, then the population would speedily multiply and the increased competition thus brought about among the laborers would depress wages again to the lowest amount sufficient to support a family. This theory of population is known as the Malthusian theory, named after its formulator. Under the name of the "iron law of wages," this theory is still put forth by the socialists, together with the institution of private property, as the explanation of wages.

THE PRODUCTIVITY THEORY

Historically, however, the Malthusian theory has been proved untrue, as the advance in the standard of living among the working class during the past century testifies. It has now been almost wholly superseded by the so-called "productivity theory," [*] which asserts that wages depend upon the productivity of labor; that the laborer gets what he produces; and that this share is assured him by the working out of the competitive process under free competition. If this theory is true, there can be no ethical question raised; if labor is dissatisfied with its share, then it must increase its productive efficiency. As a matter of fact wages have always been high in the United States because labor has been relatively scarce compared with land and capital, and consequently its marginal productivity has been high.

THE BARGAIN THEORY

The third theory says that wages are a result of bargaining, of competition in the labor market, a question of supply and demand. Under these circumstances it is largely a question of economic strength between labor and capital, and if labor is well-organized, alert, and able to drive a good bargain, then wages will be high; other-

[*] More truly, the marginal productivity theory.

wise they will be low. While there is an element of truth in the last theory, the second one seems the truest explanation of general wages; certain it is that no monopoly power of labor, however great, could permanently maintain wages at a level higher than the actual produce of labor. The element of truth in the first theory is that wages can never, for any length of time, fall below the cost of living.

INEQUALITY IN EARNING POWER

The economist is interested in the problem of functional distribution, but to the individual worker that of his own share in the social income is of greater importance. Why is it that some men receive so much more than other men? What are the causes that make for differences in earning power of different individuals? In answering this question we may first distinguish between racial and individual characteristics.

Differences in productive efficiency due apparently to racial and national variations have often been noted. For instance, Americans have been particularly efficient in the invention of labor-saving devices and the use of complicated machinery; the Germans in lines of work requiring patient, untiring industry; the French in branches where artistic design was of importance; and the Japanese in whatever called for deftness of touch. These peculiarities are not fixed or permanent, however, and the tendency is for these national differences to disappear with migration of labor and the development of technical training.

The differences between individuals of the same race or nation are even more marked than those between different nationalities. These are partly inborn and partly the result of training. We may classify the factors that make for variation as follows:

(1) Objective physical conditions, such as plentiful national resources, improved machinery and capital to work with, and good and sufficient food, clothing, and shelter to maintain efficiency at a high level; if the worker is well equipped in all these ways, he will be able to produce more than another man who is less well provided for. This is one of the explanations of high wages in the United States.

(2) A favorable political and social environment, which affords security of life and property, freedom from the burdens of militarism, honesty and commercial morality, social ideals which hold labor in respect and call forth the best efforts in each man—all of these favor the development of efficiency in the case of the worker, and the absence of any one of them handicaps him decidedly. In this group may also be included the organization and division of labor; where these are highly and skilfully developed by able managers the productive capacity of the individual worker may be greatly increased.

(3) Many of these factors lie apparently beyond the control of the individual, but we now come to a group which the individual worker may influence. His bodily strength and vigor may be increased and maintained by right living, the avoidance of dissipation and vicious habits, and the proper observance of the laws of health. But even more important in our modern industrial society with its constant demands upon the intellectual capacity of the worker, is education, and in this connection especially technical education. Every child starts life equally incapable and ignorant; the extent of the progress that he makes toward the goal of success will depend almost entirely upon the degree to which his faculties are trained

and sharpened. The importance of education of the right
sort can scarcely be overestimated.

DISTRIBUTION OF FORTUNES

Of practical and growing interest in this connection
are such problems as the increase of large fortunes, the
causes of poverty, and similar questions. The boast of
our Republic has long been that here opportunity was
open to all, that wealth was widely diffused, and that such
inequalities of fortune as characterized the nations of the
Old World were happily lacking. In the fifty-five years,
1850-1904, the per capita value of all property in the
United States exactly quadrupled; how has this increase
been distributed? Unfortunately we have no complete
statistics on this point, yet reliable estimates by authorita-
tive writers all tell the same story—of great concentration of wealth in the possession of a comparatively few
rich families. In 1893 Mr. George K. Holmes concluded
from a study of the statistics of farm and home ownership in the United States that "91 per cent of the families
of the country own no more than about 29 per cent of the
wealth, and 9 per cent of the families own about 71 per
cent of the wealth." A more accurate and satisfactory
statement can be drawn from the income-tax returns for
Prussia, which tells almost the same story with regard
to income. The following table is condensed from an article by Professor A. Wagner.

DISTRIBUTION OF INCOME IN PRUSSIA, 1902

INCOME	PER CENT OF PERSONS	PER CENT OF INCOME
Below $214	70.7	33.0
$214 to $714	25.8	34.9
Over $714	3.5	32.1

According to these figures over two-thirds of the persons—heads of families or single adults—had only one-third of the income, while 3½ per cent had another third. Another striking fact shown by the table is the large proportion of persons receiving incomes of less than $214 a year, the minimum taxable income. It shows the poverty of the mass of the people as well as the concentration of wealth among the few rich. In the United States, where the natural resources have been so much richer than in Germany, a similar table would probably show a much smaller proportion under the Prussian minimum, but on the other hand it would probably show a greater concentration of income in the hands of a few. Europe has as yet no billionaire.

Causes of Fortunes in the United States

The great fortunes of the United States have been made possible by the unrivaled opportunities for the exploitation of rich natural resources, the appropriation of natural monopolies, and by special privileges and opportunities in manufactures and transportation. The importance of monopoly privileges in the distribution of wealth is well shown by the results of an investigation made in 1892 by the New York Tribune into the sources of the fortunes of millionaires. It was undertaken to show that protection was not the main cause; but while it proved this, it showed clearly that most of them were built up on monopoly.

Of the 4,047 millionaires reported, only 1,125, or 28 per cent, obtained their fortunes in protected industries. * * * About 78 per cent of the fortunes were derived from permanent monopoly privileges, and only 22 per cent from competitive industries unaided by natural and artificial monopolies. * * *

Furthermore, if the size of fortunes is taken into account it will be found that perhaps 95 per cent of the total values represented by these millionaire fortunes is due to those investments classed as land values and natural monopolies, and to competitive industries aided by such monopolies.[5]

It is essential to the stability of our democratic institutions that all special privileges be absolutely prohibited and that monopoly be brought under strict government control and regulation. Improper methods of wealth accumulation should certainly be prevented.

TENDENCIES

The opposite question of poverty has already been discussed and some of the causes of poverty pointed out. It will be sufficient here to try to answer the question which has often been asked: Are the rich growing richer and the poor, poorer? Though the first part of the question has just been affirmed, the second part may be denied.

The nineteenth century has witnessed a vast improvement in the condition of the laboring man, who has shared in the increasing wealth which he has helped to produce. Wages have steadily increased, the hours of labor have been reduced, and the material well-being of the wage-earner is greater today than it has ever been before. It has more than once been pointed out by writers on this subject that with an equal distribution of wealth no one would be rich, while many others insist that inequality in itself is a desirable thing.

Greater diffusion of wealth can come about only by very slow processes, and permanent plenty can be secured only by a great increase in the accumulations of

5 Commons, *The Distribution of Wealth*, p. 252.

capital and the efficiency of each worker. Any suggested reform, therefore, that would weaken the motives to thrift and industry must be rejected.

TEST QUESTIONS

1. What are the three great problems of economic society?
2. What is meant by functional distribution? What four factors enter into functional distribution?
3. What is meant by personal distribution? What problems are involved?
4. Are the different factors of distribution governed by natural law? Illustrate.
5. What are the two different meanings given to the word "rent"?
6. What factors determine economic rent? What is the contention of the Socialists with respect to economic rent?
7. Why did the statesmen and church leaders in former times oppose interest?
8. Distinguish between borrowing for a productive purpose and borrowing to pay living expenses.
9. Just exactly what is the nature of interest?
10. What is meant by profits? What is Walker's theory concerning profits?
11. Do profits ever come out of wages? Explain.
12. What is meant by wages? What three theories are held concerning wages? Which seems most reasonable?
13. Name the factors that cause the economic powers of different individuals to differ from one another.
14. Explain the distribution of fortunes within the United States. What problems does it raise?

CHAPTER XVI

SAVING AND SPENDING

THE RATIONAL USE OF WEALTH

The goal and purpose of all economic activities is the satisfaction of human wants. The object of production is consumption. We work because we desire and need various things which we can get only if we produce them or earn the money to buy them. In this chapter we take up some of the problems connected with the rational use or consumption of the wealth which is continually being produced. We have seen something of the conditions under which it is produced and the manner in which it is distributed; we must now study the not less important subject of its application to human needs and desires.

The practical importance of this subject of business management is well known. Industry caters to wants. Economic activities are motivated by this fundamental principle. The steel industry, for example, has reached its present magnitude because of the enlarged demands for steel in machinery, structural work, ships, rails, steel cars, war supplies, etc. The infinite variety and amount of human desires account for the endless diversity and increasing struggle of our modern industrial society. Considered from the standpoint of consumption, this problem resolves itself into the great question: How can we get the largest and most rational return for a given expenditure?

Before trying to answer this question, it will be helpful to present a summary statement of actual expenditures in different places.

EXPENDITURES FOR DIFFERENT PURPOSES

ITEMS	UNITED STATES 1903	NEW YORK CITY	GREAT BRITAIN	PRUSSIA	AVERAGE
Food	43.1	43.4	51.4	55.0	48.2
Clothing	13.0	10.6	18.1	18.0	14.9
Rent	18.1	19.4	13.5	12.0	15.8
Fuel and light....	5.7	5.1	3.5	5.0	4.8
Miscellaneous	20.1	21.5	13.5	10.0	16.3
Total	100.0	100.0	100.0	100.0	100.0

From this table it is seen that practically half of the income of average working-class families is expended for food and five-sixths of it goes for the bare necessaries. It is therefore of the utmost importance that this be spent wisely. The remaining one-sixth, included here under the head "miscellaneous," comprises such items as education, care of health, comfort, mental and bodily recreation, etc. It is manifest that this group can be expanded in only one of two ways: either by enlarging the total income or by economizing on the other items by a wiser and better-ordered expenditure. The former question has already been discussed; here we are concerned only with the latter.

Dr. Frederick Engel, a Prussian statistician, laid down certain laws with regard to consumption. As the income of a family increases a smaller percentage is spent for food and a larger percentage for education, health, recreation, etc., while the percentage spent for clothing, rent, fuel, and light remains approximately the same. A higher civilization and culture for the mass of the people can be secured only by expanding the group of culture expenditures. As long as these remain unsatisfied for the ordinary family we cannot claim to have attained our economic goal. The author of a recent study of condi-

Fɪɢ. 10.—Distribution of a Family Income, $900 to $1,000

tions in New York City, where the cost of living is high, concludes that a "fair living wage for a workingman's family in New York City should be at least $728 a year, or a steady income of $14 a week." [1] The actual average earnings are certainly below this figure.

The table on the following page shows the average income and expenditure of a number of families in New York City as determined by actual investigation.

[1] More, *Wage-earners' Budgets*, p. 269.

INCOME AND EXPENDITURE [2]

ITEMS OF EXPENDITURE	GROUP I INCOME, $600-$699: AVERAGE, $650	GROUP II INCOME, $700-$799: AVERAGE, $748	GROUP III INCOME, $800-$899: AVERAGE, $846
Rent	$154	$161	$168
Car fare	11	10	16
Fuel and light	38	37	41
Furniture	6	8	7
Insurance	13	18	18
Food	279	314	341
Meals eaten away from home....	11	22	18
Clothing	83	99	114
Health	14	14	22
Taxes, dues, and contributions...	8	9	11
Recreation and amusement......	3	6	7
Education	5	5	7
Miscellaneous	25	32	41
Totals	$650	$735	$811

In this connection the factors that influence and determine the cost of living may be briefly summarized:

FACTORS THAT DETERMINE THE COST OF LIVING [3]

I. Cost of living includes:
   1. Economic expenditures, or such as contribute to efficiency
     a. Rent
     b. Food
     c. Clothing
     d. Fuel and light
     e. Sundries, including outlay for health, recreation, amusement, education, religion, and government

[2] Report of Special Committee on Standard of Living in New York City.
[3] Adapted from the Report of the (Massachusetts) Commission on the Cost of Living (1910).

2. Uneconomic expenditures, or such as do not contribute
   to efficiency
   A. Individual wastage
      a. Drink
      b. Luxury
      c. Amusement
      d. Domestic waste
   B. Social wastage
      a. War
      b. Governmental extravagance
      c. Crime, pauperism, insanity, accident, disease, un-
         employment, and the like

II. The cost of living should be considered not only absolutely,
    as above, but relatively, as shown by proportion of ex-
    penditures to incomes:
    1. Wages
    2. Salaries
    3. Profits
    4. Interest
    5. Leisure
    6. Idleness

III. The prices of commodities and services which constitute
     the items of expenditure classified above, are determined
     by supply, by demand, and by value of money, as fol-
     lows:
     1. Supply depends on expenses of production
        a. Natural resources and marginal productivity of land
        b. Ordinary competitive expenses
           (1) Interest on capital
           (2) Profits of management
           (3) Cost of labor, as determined by wages, hours,
               and efficiency
        c. Effects of legislation
           (1) Sanitary laws
           (2) Pure food laws
           (3) Labor laws
           (4) Tariff laws

    d. Effects of combination
      (1) Capital—trusts
      (2) Labor—unions
    e. Effects of wastage
      (1) Public and private extravagance
      (2) Planless and wasteful methods of production
         and distribution
    f. Effects of improvements and inventions
  2. Demand depends on
    a. Size and growth of population, as governed by birth
      rate, death rate, and immigration
    b. Amount of incomes
    c. Standard of living, as influenced by advance of cul-
      ture, growth of cities, custom and fashion, habits
      of spending and saving
  3. Value of money depends on
    a. Supply of gold
    b. Currency system
    c. Use of credit

Economy in Consumption

These facts emphasize the importance of economy in consumption. It is said that an American family will waste enough food for a French family to live on. The farmer who leaves his implements out in the rain or his cattle without proper shelter, is guilty of waste. We all waste clothing by frequent changes in fashion. Such waste is due as much to a lack of knowledge and training as to carelessness. The single example of the consumption of food will illustrate this point.

If we place the average income of an American family at $500—and it will not greatly exceed that figure—then nearly $250 of this amount is expended each year for food. Waste occurs in any or all of the following ways: (1) needlessly expensive foods containing little real nutriment are used; (2) there is a failure to select the foods best suited to the needs of the family; (3) a great deal is thrown away which ought to be utilized; (4) bad preparation of the food causes it to lose much of the nutriment which it does contain; (5) badly constructed ovens diffuse heat, instead of confining it, and cause enormous loss of fuel. We shall state less than the truth if we estimate that fully one-fifth of the money expended for food is absolutely wasted, while the excessive expenditure often fails to provide adequate nutrition.[6]

The remedy for such a waste as this clearly lies in the teaching of domestic science in our public schools to the daughters and future wives of the workingmen. As the ordinary household expenses, as shown above, absorb from 80 to 90 per cent of the ordinary income, the training of the housewife, under whose control they fall, is almost as imperative as that of the wage-earner.

The Relation of Consumption to Productive Efficiency

The economic evils of intemperance will be more fully stated below in the objections to luxury. There is, however, one additional objection to the excessive use of intoxicating liquor which is not true of most indulgences, and that is the fact that it diminishes a man's productive powers. It is harmful in its effects both upon consumption and upon production.

Other items of consumption appear, however, not so clearly under the immediate control of the consumer. The housing accommodations in many of our large cities have often been unsanitary and unworthy of being called homes. Legislation has been necessary to compel the

[6] Bullock, *Introduction to Study of Economics*, p. 106.

erection of better tenements and to prevent the exploitation of helpless people. So too it has been found necessary to legislate against loan-sharks, in order to protect
people against their own improvidence 'and ignorance.
In addition to legislation against positive evils, we must
of course look to education as the great remedy of waste
in consumption.

There is one other phase of the subject of consumption
that may well be mentioned before leaving this subject.
Owing to the constant pressure of the consuming public
for cheap goods, many articles are produced under conditions dangerous to the health, morality, and well-being
of the operatives, as in the case of the "sweated" trades.
To remedy these evils consumers' leagues have been
started in many places, the members of which pledge
themselves not to buy goods or to trade in stores where
the conditions of work are not up to certain prescribed
standards. They realize that as consumers they owe a
duty to other members of society not to exploit them.
While this method has proved a fairly effective method
of protest in some cases, it cannot be looked to as a complete solution óf this evil. But it emphasizes the fact that
the interests of all members of society as producers and
consumers are closely interdependent and that the progress of society requires the improvement of the condition
of all.

The Nature of Saving and Spending

One of the problems which has often proved very puz-
zling is the relation between saving and spending. At
what point should one stop spending in order to save? If
the satisfaction of our wants is the object of production,
why should we save at all? This is the point urged by the
author of a specious little book entitled *The Fallacy of*

Saving. The problem can be most easily solved by a more careful analysis of terms. In the popular view, saving involves the withdrawal of goods or money from use, while spending means putting them to immediate use. The spendthrift is proverbially popular. "If the rich do not spend, the poor die of hunger," said Montesquieu. Saving may take the form of hoarding, or withdrawing things from use, but nowadays this is practiced only by misers; saving ordinarily takes the form of investment in some productive enterprise, either directly or through a bank. In this way a demand is created for goods just as truly as though the money had been spent for a dinner or a suit of clothes. Saving is spending, but it is spending for the future rather than for the present; it usually causes the production of permanent material goods rather than transient or immaterial pleasures.

Another cause of the confusion of ideas on this subject is that we always speak of money and thus lose sight of the acts of production and consumption that lie back of the money transfer. We see that money is transferred by spending and think that it increases trade. Consequently when a prodigal spends his money foolishly, it is excused on the ground that it makes employment and puts money in circulation. We forget that it would have been put in circulation just as effectively if he had not spent it, but had placed it in a bank. If we look back of the money transfer, we see that usually there has been a foolish or wasteful expenditure, sometimes an absolute destruction of wealth. A fire which burns down valuable buildings is an absolute social loss, even though employment be given to masons and carpenters in putting them up again.

The Fallacy of Making Work

A third confusion of ideas that exists in the popular mind is due to an over-emphasis of the desirability of work for its own sake. The man who "makes work" is thought to be doing a desirable thing, even though this results from the unnecessary destruction of useful things. Now the real goal of all rational economic endeavor is not production for its own sake, but consumption; not work, but the gratification of wants. Every destruction of durable commodities which lessens the power to gratify wants is a loss to a community and no juggling with words can make it anything else. If it gives employment to labor, this means that the labor has been diverted from the production of other things to which it would have been devoted. Every year fires destroy property in the United States to the value of $250,000,000. That workmen are employed to reproduce the buildings, etc., can surely not be reckoned as a social gain. There is great danger in a commercial age like ours of forgetting that work is not an end in itself but simply a means to an end.

But it may be argued that unless these men had been given employment of this sort, they would have starved. It is conceivable that during or after a revolution, industry would be so interrupted that ordinary employments would not be open. But in ordinary times such a statement is simply an assertion of the fallacious lump-of-labor theory, that there is just so much work to be done and no more. As a matter of fact new wants are continually pressing for satisfaction, waiting only for the prior ones to be satisfied before they urge their claims. So soon as the old ones are satisfied, additional employment is provided in meeting the newer desires. The aim of society is to expand continually the circle of gratified desires. As durable goods and agents are accumulated by the process of saving, this becomes increasingly possible in every progressive society. Useless destruction involves sheer waste and cannot be justified on any grounds.

Useful Savings

On the other hand saving is socially necessary in every industrially developed community in order to furnish the requisite capital for the continued production of wealth. Professor Marshall has estimated that every year one-fifth of the wealth of a nation is used up in the processes of manufacture and production; just to keep machines, factories, railroads, and other instruments of production up to the point of efficiency and to restore loss and depreciation would therefore require considerable saving. If the nation is to grow wealthier and is to accumulate additional capital, manifestly still more must be saved. This is done in all progressive countries.

Saving is carried on by individuals, however, and not by nations, and the motives that lead to it are personal. The most important is probably the desire to provide for wife and children or other relatives; next to that is the wish to lay by sufficient for one's old age. In our individualistic society, where each family forms an independent unit and is assumed to be self-supporting, it is very desirable that habits of thrift and saving be developed. Both from a social and a personal point of view therefore saving must be approved, though it is undesirable that it should proceed so far as to prevent spending for the gratification of essential present needs.

The Waste of Luxuries

But what shall we say about expenditures for luxuries? Here the spending is for the gratification of a want, though it may be out of proportion to the results. What shall be our attitude to it? This question is not so easy to answer as the other. Three different schools have given as many answers to the problem of luxury. The first condemns it utterly; the second approves it wholly; and the third takes an intermediate position.

Luxury is condemned by the first school of thinkers from three points of view: (1) As a question of individual morals it is regarded as debasing and enervating, thus preventing the highest development of the human faculties; (2) as a question of economics it is condemned as wasteful; and (3) as a question of right and justice it is incompatible with an equitable distribution of wealth. It is upon this last point that the opponents of luxury lay the greatest emphasis. As the quantity of existing wealth is insufficient to satisfy even the primal wants of the large majority of our fellow-creatures, we should endeavor to increase this available store as much as we can and should refrain from drawing upon it in a reckless manner in order to gratify superfluous wants. Furthermore the productive powers that we can use are, as a matter of fact, limited; and therefore if the wealthy classes divert a portion of these forces toward the production of articles of luxury, there will be so much the less available for the production of those staple articles that the masses require for their consumption.

In the case of a Robinson Crusoe this would be clear. If he devoted several months to the polishing of a diamond for ornament, he would have to go without a house or other improvements he might have made in that time. Or if he forced his man Friday to spend half his time polishing diamonds for him, Friday might be compelled to go without sufficient clothing or food or housing. The same thing is true of organized society, only the truth is

hidden by the phenomena of exchange. It has been estimated [4] that the annual consumption of wealth in the
United States is divided somewhat as follows: necessaries, six billion dollars; luxuries, three and one-half billion (of which nine hundred million dollars go for liquor
and five hundred million dollars for tobacco); capitalistic
uses, three and three-quarter billion. It is manifest that
if the expenditure for luxuries were curtailed or abandoned, there would be more to devote to the other
categories.

The Need of Luxuries

The opposite school replies to these arguments that
luxury is an indispensable stimulus to progress; that
really all economic progress is first manifested in the
form of a need of luxury, and that luxury therefore is a
necessary phase of its development. Since luxury is
wholly relative, every want or need is, on its first appear-
ance in the world, regarded as superfluous (1) because
no one has hitherto wanted it, and (2) because its production probably requires a considerable amount of labor,
on account of man's experience and the inevitable grop-
ings in the dark that attend all beginnings. The decen-
cies of life today and even the necessities were once regarded as luxuries—chimneys in houses, shoes, forks and
knives, linen for the body, bath tubs, etc. If all luxury
had always been sternly suppressed when it made its ap-
pearance, all the needs that constitute civilization would
have been nipped in the bud, and we should still be in the
condition of our ancestors of the Stone Age. Civilization
depends on the multiplication of wants. Economic prog-

[4] Gide, *Political Economy*, Rev. Ed., p. 663.

ress is a process of converting superfluities into conveniences and conveniences into necessities.

THE INTERMEDIATE VIEW

The attitude taken by practically all economists today is intermediate between these two extremes. Moderate luxury is justified, but lavish and indiscriminate luxury is disapproved. This justification of luxury rests upon purely economic grounds. In so far as personal consumption is the objective point of production, the prohibition of luxury would act as an impediment to enterprise. If the desire to enjoy luxuries stimulates the productive powers of economically important members of society, it is justifiable as a necessary motive force.

The introduction of luxuries and the consequent raising of the standard of living seem often the only way to secure progress. If the mass of the people live on the minimum of cheap food, multiply as long as cheap food is to be had, and spend little for comforts and luxuries, then most of the labor of such a community must be spent in obtaining food for the masses. Such is the condition in India and China. But if a large part of the community has a higher standard of living, it will exercise self-restraint in the increase of its numbers, and the whole level of intelligence and comfort will be raised, as is the case in France, Switzerland, and New England.

On the other hand, it is urged that "failure on the part of any family to secure the necessaries of life is injurious, not only to it, but to the whole community. Under-consumption means under-nutrition and loss in industrial efficiency. If permitted to continue it must inevitably undermine the standards which make a family self-supporting and self-sufficient and reduce its members to dependency. The general interest requires, therefore, acceptance of the maxim: the consumption of luxuries should be deferred until all are provided with necessaries. * * * This suggests that no one is justified in spending income for a luxury for himself or his family that will afford less happiness than would the same income spent for someone else.'' [5]

The Socialization of Wealth

But the difficult question at once suggests itself: How can the surplus incomes of the rich be used so as to provide for the needs of the poor, without undermining their independence or permanently lowering their earning power? It has been suggested that there should be a socialization of luxury; that the rich should use their wealth for the construction of public art galleries, libraries, parks, baths, etc., which would thus gratify as great a number as possible. The feeling is growing in the United States and in the world that wealth is a social trust and that the ownership of wealth imposes upon a person certain moral obligations. While every man has a legal right to spend his surplus income as he pleases, he is morally bound to spend it in such a way as to increase the welfare of the whole community.

TEST QUESTIONS

1. What is the main purpose of all economic activities?

2. In their order of importance, what are the chief items in the expenditure of family incomes? How do these proportions vary with different incomes?

3. What are the chief economic expenditures in the cost-of-living problem? What are the chief uneconomic expenditures?

4. What three factors determine the prices of commodities?

---

[5] Seager, *Principles of Economics*, p. 80.

5. Which factor has been most influential in determining the rising cost of living in the United States during the years 1895-1910? Explain.

6. What is meant by saving? How does it differ from hoarding?

7. What is the economic fallacy in the making-work argument?

8. About how much of the wealth of a country is annually destroyed in the processes of manufacture and production? How is it replaced?

9. Mention some desirable economies in consumption.

10. What is the relation of consumption to productive efficiency?

11. What arguments are put forth condemning luxury?

12. What arguments are advanced to show that luxury is an indispensable stimulus to progress?

13. What is the rational attitude toward luxuries?

CHAPTER XVII

TAXATION AND TARIFF

THE NATURE OF TAXES

In no way does the state affect the interests of its citizens more vitally than in the sphere of taxation. The state in modern society is the people organized for certain collective purposes, as for the public defense, the preservation of domestic peace, and the furtherance of social and industrial welfare. To carry out these objects money is needed and the state has therefore to collect from its citizens sufficient revenue to defray its expenditures. John Fiske has tersely defined taxes as "portions of private property taken for public purposes." Taxation thus implies a certain degree of compulsion; by it the government interferes with the free choice of the individual and expends a part at least of his income for him in ways that he himself might not have chosen. The social and industrial consequences of a system of taxation may also be far-reaching and important. As Professor R. T. Ely says:

Taxation may create monopolies, or it may prevent them; it may diffuse wealth, or it may control it; it may promote labor or equality of rights, or it may tend to the establishment of tyranny and despotism; it may be used to bring about reform, or it may be used to aggravate existing grievances and foster dissensions between classes.

231

It is evident therefore that the utmost care should be exercised in framing a system of taxation.

RULES OF TAXATION

Certain canons or rules of taxation were laid down by Adam Smith over a hundred years ago and have been generally endorsed by economists ever since. One was that taxes ought to be certain and not arbitrary as to amount, time, and manner of payment; another was that taxes ought to be levied in the manner most convenient to the tax-payer; and a third, that taxes ought to take as little as possible out of the pockets of the tax-payer over and above what is paid into the public treasury. These three maxims—certainty, convenience, and economy— have been generally accepted, but less general agreement exists in regard to the fourth, which states that the subjects of every state ought to contribute to the support of the government as nearly as possible in proportion to their respective abilities.

This rule has given rise to two problems: Is ability the most just basis of taxation? If so, how is ability to be measured? The theory of justice generally accepted by legal writers and by the American courts is expressed in the maxim that taxes should be proportioned to benefits received. The benefit theory affords a good rule in the assessment of local property taxes, but fails utterly in the domain of national and state affairs. Who can measure the benefits to each individual of an appropriation for a new warship or for a state penitentiary or for the public school system?

Probably the benefits are in inverse proportion to the income or wealth of the individual, and the heaviest taxes would then have to be apportioned to those least able to pay. Most economists today agree that taxes should be apportioned according to "faculty" or ability to pay. It satisfies better our sense of fairness and is more readily applicable than the benefit theory. In the last analysis, of course, it may be said that taxation in general must confer real benefits upon society or it will not be tolerated. Here, however, we are concerned with a rule of apportionment.

BASES OF TAXATION

The second practical problem encountered is when we attempt to apply the faculty principle in practice. How is ability to be measured? Three measures have been suggested: expenditure, income, and property. Taxation on expenditure is open to the objection that it would place an unduly large proportion of the tax burdens on the poor, whose expenditures are larger in proportion to their means than those of other classes of society. To make property the sole base of taxation is objectionable because large classes of society, including professional men with large incomes, would then escape taxation largely or altogether. Income, on the surface, seems the fairest measure of ability, but is objectionable because the incomes of different individuals, both on account of source and size, really indicate unequal and dissimilar abilities. In practice, however, all three methods are employed in all advanced states; so it is not necessary to decide which is theoretically the fairest.

PROGRESSIVE TAXES

Still another practical question confronts us after we adopt the ability theory: Shall the rate of taxation be the same no matter what the amount of the property or income, or shall it increase as the amount grows larger? In other words, shall taxation be proportional or progressive? In general the advocates of the ability theory also support progression, though there are many exceptions to this statement. Three main arguments have been urged in support of this method.

First, progression is advocated in order to secure equality of sacrifice; it is argued that each dollar of a $10,000 income affords less gratification to the owner than each dollar of a $1,000 income, and that consequently in order to equalize the sacrifices of the two individuals a larger proportion of the first income should be taken than of the second. However, the objection to this is that wants expand even more rapidly than incomes and therefore the initial assumption is untrue.

Progression is urged, in the second place, by those who desire to use taxation as a method of introducing social reforms or of bringing about a more equitable distribution of wealth, as by the breaking up of large fortunes. It seems inadvisable, however, to use the machinery of taxation for such purposes.

Other writers urge that the ability to earn or produce wealth increases at an accelerating rate, and that taxation should therefore keep pace with it. "It is the first thousand that counts." The objection is made here that it would penalize ability and energy.

In general, while the arguments are not conclusive, progression certainly secures a nearer approach to the ideal of the ability theory than does proportional taxation. The practical application, after we accept it, is still a difficult matter. It should be applied to the revenue system as a whole by the careful selection of special taxes. As a matter of fact we have just the opposite system in the United States, for the poor man undoubtedly pays out a larger proportion of his income in taxes—principally on articles of consumption—than do his wealthy neighbors. This condition has been somewhat modified by the use of the income tax.

Direct and Indirect Taxes

In the main there has been a clear division in the United States between the sources of income of the federal government on the one hand and those of the state and local governments on the other. The federal treasury has derived its revenue almost entirely from indirect taxes—excise and customs, while the other governments have depended chiefly upon direct taxes upon persons, property, business, corporations, and inheritances. The division rests upon the constitutional allotment of powers, but it also corresponds very closely to the industrial and political functions of each in their relations to the individual citizens. The chief duty of the federal government is that of national defense and foreign intercourse, relations which are national in extent but which affect the individual only remotely; so, too, its taxing area is national and its exactions are felt only distantly. Few persons, it has been said, taste the tax in their tea or their whisky, yet over one-third of all the taxes collected in the United States are derived from either customs or excise duties. Whisky and tobacco contribute most of the internal revenue, while import duties are levied on practically everything brought into the country which could compete with any home product. These two sources yield over $600,000,000 a year to the federal treasury.

During the Civil War the sources of revenue of the country were supplemented by a Federal Income Tax, which remained in operation until 1872. Such a law was again passed in 1893, but was declared unconstitutional by the Supreme Court. The constitution has since been amended to grant the federal government the power to levy an income tax and such a tax has been established to supplement the revenue derived from indirect sources. An income tax is generally approved of by taxing authorities, because it is an elastic tax. The rates can easily be modified to meet the financial needs of the government without upsetting business in the same manner as would be done by a revision of the tariff rates to meet the demands of the treasury. It is generally admitted that a tariff and an excise tax are too fluctuating to be dependable. A shock to business will result in an enormous decrease in revenue. To attempt to adjust the tariff rates accordingly at such a time would only add to the confusion. The effect of a slight change in the rate of an income tax does not have this far-reaching effect upon business and at the same time keeps the revenues of the government steadier.

THE GENERAL PROPERTY TAX

The main reliance of the state and local governments in this country is the general property tax, which amounted in 1902 to over $700,000,000, or almost half of all the taxes collected. This really consists of two very distinct parts, which present quite different problems, namely, the tax on real estate and that on personal property. Under our peculiar system by which property is assessed locally and upon the basis of that assessment its share of the state taxes apportioned to each locality, there is every incentive offered to the local assessor to undervalue the land in his jurisdiction, thereby escaping part of the state burdens. This evil of inequality between localities could be obviated by the simple expedient of exempting real estate from all state taxes and leaving it solely to the counties and cities for purposes of taxation.

In the case of personal property the great evil is evasion. Much of our modern wealth exists in the form of securities, stocks, bonds, mortgages, etc., and this is practically undiscoverable by assessors, except by the voluntary declaration of the tax-payer. This is truthfully made only by trustees and a few conscientious persons. Most of our laws have been directed to the discovery of this intangible property as it is called, but without avail. In a few of the most progressive states the effort has at last been recognized as futile, and the attempt is now being made to reach these sources of income indirectly, by taxes on corporations, on business, franchises, and other tangible evidences of wealth.

Inheritance Taxes

Not only are corporation, business, license, and similar taxes being developed, but increasing resort is had to inheritance taxes, over thirty states now making use of this form of taxation. They usually fall more heavily on collateral than on direct inheritances, and in many states are progressive both as to amount and as to nearness of relationship. Thus in Wisconsin the rates advance from 1 per cent for bequests under $25,000 to husband, wife, or lineal relation, to 15 per cent for sums over $500,000 to very distant relatives or strangers. These various forms of taxation are necessary to secure the needed revenues for the state governments, especially if these forego further resort to taxation of realty.

The tendency is now sufficiently marked to make it possible to indicate with some certainty the future of taxation in this country. To a certain extent, however, this must be regarded as the expression of an ideal rather than the description of an existing system. The federal government should have customs and excise duties, supplemented by an income tax. The state governments should have corporation and inheritance taxes. The cities and minor civil divisions should have taxes on realty, with license and franchise taxes. Such a division is logical and avoids duplication of taxation of the same source by two or more grades of government.

GROWTH OF PUBLIC DEBTS

Other problems connected with finance are suggested in connection with the universal tendency to increase governmental expenditures and public debts. The former is an expression of the growth and expansion of state functions, which will be discussed in the next chapter. The latter is due in part to this same fact, in part also to the development of credit and the creation of a market for the sale of public and other securities, and finally to the growth of constitutional government, which has made the people willing to entrust their capital to a government which they themselves as citizens really control.

THE TARIFF

The question of tariff involves such important economic as well as financial consideration that it seems best to discuss this form of taxation somewhat more fully. It has been used not merely as a means of raising revenue but also as an instrument to develop particular industries and to prevent foreign competition. Any detailed discussion of this subject therefore involves a statement of the pros and cons of protection and free trade. It should be said, however, in advance that the real issue is not free trade, for that is demanded by only a few doctrinaires, but freer trade through intelligent adjustments of the tariff. The system of protection has prevailed in the

United States for virtually one hundred years, and could not be suddenly changed and abolished if desired. From the financial standpoint, too, import duties are absolutely essential to the support of our federal government; the question here is not absolutely free trade, but the choice of articles for revenue purposes. Shall they be those which are not produced in this country or those which enter into competition with domestic products? If financial considerations alone prevailed, the former would undoubtedly be selected as the more convenient, certain, and economical. But in the determination of the tariff policies of the United States economic considerations have been paramount and to an examination of these we must now turn.

ARGUMENTS FOR PROTECTION

Historically the following arguments have played the main role in support of protection at different times in the United States. The infant industries argument was advanced by Hamilton in his celebrated Report on Manufactures in 1791 and has always been important until recently, when the infants had grown to be so lusty that evidently more valid reasons for protecting them must be discovered. This was found in the plea for diversified production, which was necessary for a well-rounded economic development; the need of creating a strong national government and national spirit also played its part. In order to win over the farmers the home market argument was early urged; this has taken various forms. In the first place it was argued that the building up of manufacturing centers and the consequent increase in population would give the farmers a better market than the fluctuating foreign one. As set forth by Carey, it would keep within the country the elements taken from the soil. It would also save the freights on the transportation of goods back and forth across the ocean. Each of these arguments has lost force with the development of the country and the decrease in the cost of transportation.

More important today is the wages argument; at first protection was urged because wages were high in the United States and the manufacturer needed to be protected against his foreign competitor who employed cheap labor. Today it is argued that protection has raised wages and must be continued in order to protect the laborer against the pauper labor of Europe. Curiously enough, in France protection is urged for French workmen against the highly paid and efficient American. The effect of the tariff on wages has been greatly exaggerated; wages are high in the United States because the productivity of labor is high. Indeed so far as the tariff raises prices it may be argued that the real wages of labor are lowered.

More generally accepted as defensible grounds for protection are the political arguments that a nation should be able to produce its own military armaments and supplies, and that it should be able to use the tariff as a retaliatory measure. Recently this latter has received considerable force from the practice of "dumping," by which is meant the occasional sale of products abroad at prices lower than those charged at home. Domestic manufacturers in the country thus treated are of course seriously injured and have insisted upon protection against this procedure, which has been authorized in Canada.

ARGUMENTS AGAINST PROTECTION

In answer to these various arguments the free traders, or those desiring a modification of present high rates, make their main appeal to the doctrine of comparative costs. Briefly stated this asserts that nations, like individuals, can do some things better than others. Like the individual lawyer therefore who pays to have his boots blacked while he devotes himself to the law, the nation should produce the things it is best fitted for and pay others to produce other things which it can do less well. In this way each will obtain the largest possible return. Protection, which interferes with this natural international division of labor, simply diverts labor and capital from more profitable industries. Practically, this purely abstract economic argument has had little influence on the commercial policy of nations, which have been moved more by political and industrial considerations. Today, however, there is no question but that the freer movement of capital and industry throughout the world would be advantageous.

In answer to the home market argument it is pointed out that with the growth of large-scale production the profitable area of manufacture has greatly widened and now in many cases transcends national boundaries. As home producers seek foreign markets, which they are beginning to do, they themselves will demand a reduction of the tariff, especially in the matter of raw materials. Free traders also deny the need of artificially diversifying industry in a country as large and varied as the United States, or of building up infant industries. Indeed on the latter point they urge that many of our trusts are the result of the tariff, and that the attempt to grant legislative favors has resulted only in wholesale demoralization and a debauching of our national politics.

CONCLUSION

In conclusion it may be said that under certain conditions the policy of protection is relatively defensible;

that it has undoubtedly hastened the industrial development of the United States, though it has not caused it;
and that, on the other hand, it is responsible for not a
few evils in our political and industrial life. The struggle of particular interests during the framing of the
Payne bill shows the impossibility of deciding this issue
upon academic grounds. It may be prophesied, however,
that as our manufacturers reach out more seriously after
the foreign markets, the tariff will be modified so as to
make this possible.

TEST QUESTIONS

1. What is John Fiske's definition of a tax?
2. What limits are there to the power of taxation which a
government possesses?
3. What are three maxims according to which taxes should
be levied?
4. Why should taxes be levied according to the ability to pay?
Illustrate.
5. What three means are usually used in determining ability
to pay?
6. What are the arguments supporting progressive taxation?
7. What is the distinction between direct and indirect taxes?
Give an example of each.
8. From what sources does the federal government derive its
revenue?
9. What are the chief difficulties with the personal property
tax?
10. What are the leading characteristics and uses of the inheritance tax?
11. What are the leading arguments for a protective tariff?
12. What are the leading arguments against protection?
13. What are the chief points in favor of an income tax for
federal taxation?

CHAPTER XVIII

THE PRIMARY FUNCTIONS OF THE STATE

In the course of the preceding pages we have repeatedly referred to the necessity or desirability of governmental action, and have emphasized the important part which it plays in our economic life today. Every practical economic problem that confronts us calls in some degree for the exercise of state activity. It is necessary for us then, if we are to render sound judgment on these questions, to have a clear opinion as to the proper sphere of government action, as to how far the state should interfere in the economic activities of private individuals. We cannot do better than to state first the main functions of a modern state.

The modern industrial system, as we saw in the first chapter, is based upon certain fundamental institutions—personal liberty, competition, and private property. The first function of government is to guarantee to every individual the rights of freedom, property, and contract; this involves the maintenance of peace and order. These are often spoken of as "natural rights"; rather they are rational rights, based upon expediency and human welfare and created and maintained by society. Without the constant support and intervention of government they would possess little reality or significance. But in addition to guaranteeing these fundamental insti-

243

tutions, modern governments grant individuals certain privileges, as patents, copyrights, trade-marks, franchises, etc., designed to stimulate the economic activity of individuals.

THE REGULATIVE FUNCTIONS OF THE STATE

A second group of functions undertaken by the modern state is regulative. As we have seen, laws are made regulating the freedom of contract, the conditions of labor, the conduct of business, methods of banking and transportation, etc. The terms under which competitive business may be conducted are laid down, and while freedom of industry prevails for every individual it is only on condition that he conforms to the rules of the game thus prescribed. But the conditions are not merely restrictive; sometimes they are designed to promote enterprise, as in the case of gifts, subsidies, protective duties, etc. In all these ways the state interferes with the action of perfectly free competition for the purpose of securing better or more equitable conditions.

THE ECONOMIC FUNCTIONS OF THE STATE

A third group of functions embraces the direct participation in industry by the government itself, as the post-office, gas, electric, waterworks, canals, roads, sewers, parks, etc. In other countries, where the functions of government are more extended than in the United States, it conducts railroads, telegraph and telephone systems, tenements, pawnshops, theaters, industrial insurance, and various other activities. The line which divides public from private enterprise varies greatly in different countries.

Limits of State Action

This raises the general question: How far is it desirable that the economic functions of government should extend? As to the necessity of state activity in some form there can be no doubt. Production, exchange, distribution, and, to a smaller extent, consumption are all social processes; they concern the whole of society and must be brought under social control. In the middle of the eighteenth century Montesquieu laid down the proposition that taxes invariably increase with the growth of liberty. Historically this has been verified. The development of freedom in government and industry has meant the realization of self-restraint by the imposition of regulative law. But the modern state has gone further than this. It has realized the necessity of taking an active part in modern industrial life, for the equalization of the terms of competition, the redress of grievances and the furnishing of utilities, either because it could do it better or because it was the only agency capable of acting.

The standpoint of this treatise has been one of moderate individualism, believing in free competition and individual initiative, but not frightened off by the bogey of socialism, if at any point the interference of government seemed desirable or necessary. To present the matter clearly it will be well to state briefly the main theories that have been held as to the proper function of government, arranging them in their logical, though not in their historical, order.

Anarchism

At one extreme stands anarchism, which must be thought of not as anarchy and riot, but as a philosophical theory of society. Scientific anarchism contemplates an ideal state of perfect freedom, in which the state, the coercive exercise of authority by man over man, would not exist. According to this theory only the individual has rights; there is no more divinity of right in a majority than there is in kings. Government is an invasion of the right of the individual to do as he pleases, and should be abolished; with its abolition would vanish the various moral, social, and industrial evils to which it has given rise, and human society would develop on a higher plane. Stated in its extreme form anarchism is evidently too ideal for frail human nature as at present constituted.

EXTREME INDIVIDUALISM

Of more practical importance has been the theory of extreme individualism as set forth by Herbert Spencer— a view designated by Huxley as the night-watchman theory of the state. According to this the functions of government should be limited to the protection of life and property and the enforcement of contracts, but should not include such things as education, regulation of industry, local improvements, charities, coinage, etc. Private initiative and competition are trusted to supply these things, while the economic harmony of the interests of each individual with those of society will prevent any wrong from being done. The keynote of the whole theory lies in the view that government is an evil, though a necessary one, and should consequently be restricted. Adam Smith's system of natural liberty went somewhat further, as it added to the three functions named above, the construction of public works and buildings, etc.; but it excluded such activities as education and the civil courts, which we regard as most suited to government management. This theory had its origin in the reaction against the undue interference with industry by the government under mercantilism and had thus a historic justification and value.

MODIFIED INDIVIDUALISM

The theory most generally held by economists and writers in the United States is probably the modified individualism set forth by John Stuart Mill. According to him, freedom of industry ''should be the general practice; every departure from it, unless required by some great good, is a certain evil.'' Industry, he said, should be left to individuals and the government should never interfere unless there is an antagonism between social and private interests. Individuals following their own interests will always conduct business better than the government, which is inefficient, corrupt, and can fall back on taxation to cover its mistakes. Individualism should therefore be the rule and governmental action should be the exception. But Mill himself admitted that there was no theoretical limit to the extension of governmental functions, and in so doing is said to have opened the door to socialism. Nevertheless the basic idea is still that government is an evil and an extension of its activities is on the whole undesirable.

THE CULTURE STATE THEORY

Opposed to this view is the culture state theory, enunciated by Roscher and very generally held in Germany, which regards the state as a beneficent, positive, and constructive force in our industrial life. The advocates of this theory point out that the functions of the government change with progress, and that in our complex modern industrial life it should seek to improve conditions positively and not leave the people to the mercies of a blind competitive struggle; practically, it should regulate industry, conditions of work, housing, etc., and should manage all public utilities which affect the life or well-being of the citizens, as railroads, telegraphs, industrial insurance, etc.

Still further in the same direction goes the view known as state socialism, of which the best-known advocate is Professor Adolph Wagner. This advocates individualism, but insists that it is responsible for many injustices and evils, which it is consequently the duty of the state to redress. For instance the state should correct the inequalities of wealth brought about by the distribution of the social income under the present competitive system; this should be done by the progressive taxation of inheritances and incomes, the limitation of inheritance and bequest, the government ownership of public utilities, as railroads, telegraphs, telephones, coal mines, etc.

This theory stops just short of socialism, but enlarges the functions of the state to the largest degree compatible with individualism. Beyond this, and at the farthest extreme from anarchism, stands socialism, which, however, demands a more careful examination than the other views have received, because of its present prominence.

SOCIALISM

Socialism may be briefly defined in the words of Professor Ely [1] as "that contemplated system of industrial society which proposes the abolition of private property in the great material instruments of production, and the substitution therefor of collective property; and advocates the collective management of production, together with the distribution of social income by society, and pri-

---

[1] *Socialism and Social Reform*, p. 19.

vate property in the larger proportion of this social income.'' Four features are involved in this definition, namely, (1) common ownership, (2) production, (3) distribution, and (4) private incomes.

The cardinal and distinctive element in socialism is the collective or social ownership of the means of production, that is, of the land and capital. Instead of being owned privately as today, they would be owned by the people as a whole, by the state, and used by it for production. Socialists do not oppose capital, as is often said, but only the private ownership of capital. But under such a system private business as we know it today, individual enterprise for the sake of profit, could not exist. It is often urged that socialism means a ''grand divide,'' and that in such an event the shrewder and more thrifty would shortly have the wealth of the idle or stupid members of society. But just that is guarded against under socialism, for there would be no private ownership of capital, and hence no one could get his neighbor's share; it would all be held under collective ownership. With the abolition of private capital, there would disappear of course all the economic institutions that have grown up around it, as credit, banking, lease, hire, the stock and produce exchanges, etc.

COLLECTIVE MANAGEMENT OF PRODUCTION

Socialism also means the collective or social organization and management of industry. Socialists criticize severely our present methods of production, which they call planless and wasteful. They point to the constant recurrence of crises as an evidence of mistakes of the competitive system, which they say could be obviated under a well-organized comprehensive scheme. They also urge the wastes of modern capitalism in the duplication of

plants, advertising (which amounts to more than $500,-
000,000 a year in the United States), traveling salesmen,
multiplication of small stores, etc. Finally, an artificial
disharmony between the interests of society and private
individuals is promoted by our system of private property and profit. A coal trust limits the supply, farmers
rejoice over small crops, and planters used to burn part
of their cotton, in short the bounty of nature is regarded
as a calamity.

Some truth may be admitted in these criticisms, but
in answer it may be said that some of them are being
corrected under individualism, while as to those that
remain the remedy offered is worse than the disease.
The first and fundamental question is the effect of socialism on the amount produced, for, as we have seen, any
diminution would mean a worse economic condition of
society, even though it were offset by a more equal distribution. Under individualism the appeal to industry
and thrift is the self-interest of the individual, and under
the stimulus of this motive the production of wealth has
been increased enormously. It is doubtful whether the
motives of altruism, desire for social approbation, and
similar ones suggested by the socialists would promote
industrial activity as efficiently as the individualistic desire for pecuniary gain.

DIFFICULTIES OF COLLECTIVE MANAGEMENT

Moreover the difficulties of organizing and managing
all industries would be enormous. According to the socialist plan, statistics of consumption would be gathered
in advance, the idle changes of fashion would of course
disappear, and production could be accurately calculated.
But aside from the problem of securing an honest and efficient administration, the work of organizing industry

from a centralized bureau would probably prove insurmountable. The distribution of the labor force among various employments suggests another difficulty. Under individualism the necessary distribution takes place through the agency of wage payments and the choice of an occupation is left free to the individual. As the wage system would disappear with the abolition of private capital, some other means would have to be devised, as allotment by the government. But more important would be the selection of the managers of industry; competition provides a process whereby the inefficient are eliminated and the able put in charge. As socialism would be an industrial democracy the selection of the captains of industry under that system would probably be made by election. Is it likely that the voters would place over themselves the ablest, that is the strictest, most economical, and most energetic man? Taking men as we find them today, this may well be doubted.

SOCIALISM AS A SCHEME OF DISTRIBUTION

But it is as a scheme of distribution that socialism has been most warmly urged. The inequalities and injustices of present methods are pointed out and a more just system demanded. Socialists themselves, however, are not agreed as to what constitutes justice. Needs and merits have both been urged as bases of distribution, but they suffer from vagueness and difficulty in administration; most socialists today agree that equality of income would best meet the requirements of justice. They claim that talented persons have been endowed by nature with their abilities and should use them as a trust for society and not expect greater rewards than their less talented brothers. To this individualists answer that the practical question is how to secure the greatest exercise of these gifts, and that is now done by appealing to the motive of self-interest. Some writers go even further and assert that the desire for inequality is the chief stimulus to invention and enterprise.

A crucial point in every socialistic scheme is the determination of value under such a system; most socialists follow Marx and say that this should be determined by the "socially necessary labor time" required for the production of an article. Such a measure leaves out of account entirely the aspect of utility or demand, and would clearly be inadequate. Prices would be fixed by the state and calculated in labor time—most probably represented by labor checks, which would constitute the medium of exchange in the socialistic society.

SOCIALISM PERMITS PRIVATE INCOMES

Finally, in the definition given above, it was stated that private property would exist in the larger proportion of the social income after it was divided. There is no reason why this should not be true, for, though private capital would be abolished, the state would not interfere with the individual in the use of his income after it was earned. If one man preferred fine clothes and another pictures and books, it would be possible for the latter person to accumulate such articles of enjoyment or consumption. He could even have tools for private carpentering or a horse for riding, but under no circumstances would he be permitted to use these for production or as instruments of private gain. Socialism must stand or fall as a system of production and distribution; it is not necessary to criticise minor points. On these broad grounds it must be rejected, although it may fairly be admitted that socialists have often proved themselves keen and useful critics of existing institutions.

THE SINGLE TAX

Many persons in this and other countries, who do not approve of socialism, nevertheless believe in the extension of state ownership or activity along particular lines. Thus Henry George, though in other respects an individualist, did not believe in the private ownership of land. Land is limited in quantity and yields, because of its monopoly character, an "unearned increment" or rent, quite apart from the return due the owner for improvements. He proposed that the government should confiscate this unearned increment by levying a single tax on all land equal to it. He thought that this would provide revenue sufficient for all government needs without resorting to other forms of taxation; in this he was undoubtedly mistaken, but the main interest in the scheme for us is economic, and not financial. The reason for the scheme was that land, being a limited monopoly, would be increasingly in demand as society progressed, and that consequently the landlords would absorb in their increased rents most of the enlarged production of the future. This assumes that rents always increase and never decrease, which is historically untrue. Nor does the growth and progress of society necessarily increase the demand for land; it may be directed to other things, while improvements in the art of agriculture may actually decrease this demand. We must, however, admit that there are many instances of unearned increments, not only in the case of ground rents, but also of monopoly profits from various sources; these might very properly be secured to society by means of special and heavy taxes.

PUBLIC OWNERSHIP

The nationalization of the railroads and telegraph and the municipalization of local public utilities have been advocated by many persons who are not socialists, except in so far as they desire an extension of governmental activity along these lines. They urge this because the utilities in question—gas, water, electricity, telephone, street railways, etc.—are by their very nature monopolies, and because under private control they are often inefficiently or dishonestly managed. A less drastic remedy for these abuses might of course be found in regulation. Unrestricted private control of municipal monopolies is advocated by few; the real issue is between public regulation and public management. And this issue will depend in the last analysis upon the question as to which can give the best results to society.

TEST QUESTIONS

1. What are the primary functions of a state?
2. How do the regulative functions of a state differ from the primary? Give some examples of the regulative functions.
3. What is meant by the economic functions of the state? Mention some of them.
4. What is the theory of anarchism? What does it hope to accomplish?
5. What is meant by the theory of individualism?
6. What political doctrines of today may be considered a part of the individualistic school? Name some of them.
7. What is meant by the culture state theory?
8. What is meant by socialism?
9. What are four features involved in socialism?
10. Enumerate the socialists' criticisms of our present system of industrial organization.
11. Does socialism permit private incomes? Explain.
12. Give the essentials of the single tax theory.
13. To what extent has public ownership advanced in industrial affairs?
14. What factors ultimately determine the kind of industrial organization that is to prevail?

CHAPTER XIX

ECONOMIC PROGRESS

PROGRESS IN THE FIELD OF LABOR

At the conclusion of a study of this character we are inevitably led to summarize our deductions and to try to answer the question as to what the lessons of the past have taught us. In what direction are the forces of economic life taking us? The conclusion of this book is that they are making for economic progress, and it will be worth while to justify as far as possible this belief. It is, however, impossible to do this except in very general terms, for definite data for measuring this improvement do not exist, and economic progress itself is a somewhat vague conception.

Even such comparatively simple facts as the rate of wages or the hours of labor can be stated only very generally. But both of these show a decided improvement in the condition of the working class. A careful investigation for Great Britain by Mr. A. L. Bowley [1] shows that if wages for the decade 1890-1900 be represented as 100, then the course of wages during the nineteenth century would have run somewhat as follows:

[1] *Wages in the United Kingdom in the Nineteenth Century.*

Decade	Relative Wages	Decade	Relative Wages
1800-10	55-65	1850-60	65
1810-20	65-70	1860-70	75
1820-30	65	1870-80	95
1830-40	60	1880-90	90
1840-50	60	1890-1900	100

Without investigating the validity of the figures too closely, it may safely be affirmed that the movement of wages has been distinctly upward and that the rise was certainly not less than 50 per cent. For the United States the increase has not been so great, probably because wages started at a higher level. According to the Aldrich report, if wages and prices in 1860 in the United States be taken as 100, relative wages in 1840 were 82.5 and relative prices 98.5; in 1880 they were respectively 143 and 103.4; in 1903 they were 187 and 103. That is to say, relative wages showed a marked advance and real wages, owing to the fact that general prices remained almost stationary, an even greater improvement. So, too, the hours of labor appear to have been shortened in Great Britain about two hours a day (from ten to fourteen hours to from eight to twelve), and in the United States probably as much, the average length of the working day in certain employments decreasing from 10.3 hours in 1880 to 9.6 hours in 1903.

Progress in Production

In the field of production the most dramatic and striking advances have been achieved. The application of steam and more recently of electricity as the motive power for the newly invented and constantly improved machinery has permitted an enormous expansion of production. This has been made still greater by the opening up of new mines and new lands and improvements in the machinery of transportation and exchange and in the organization of business. Especially in the United States, where the natural resources were unusually rich and the people energetic and ingenious, has the growth of wealth been marvelous. And yet almost a century after the beginning of the Industrial Revolution in England, Mill alleged that labor-saving inventions had not lightened the toil of any human being; they had only enabled a greater number to live the same life of drudgery and imprisonment. What answer can we make to this indictment today? Why is it that the working class still has so little of this vast increase of wealth and still lives so close to the border line of poverty?

Problems in Distribution

To answer this question thoroughly would require an analysis of the subject of distribution, but a few reasons may be briefly suggested.[2] While the social income has been greatly increased by these improvements the amount paid in rent to owners of land, water powers, etc., has also grown. If we approve of private property in land as best adapted to stimulate its use for society, then we must admit the justice of rent and of its payment to present landowners. Similarly, too, the payment of interest to the owners of capital has absorbed a large part of the increased income of society, though the proportion going to this factor is probably growing smaller because of the fall in the rate of interest.

[2] Acknowledgment should be made at this point of indebtedness to the excellent final chapter in Prof. Seager's *Introduction to Economics.*

But as we have seen, modern industry is essentially capitalistic, that is, it depends upon the use of capital for its operations. Since we allow private property in capital and believe that to be the best method yet devised for securing its accumulation, we must justify interest. Profits in general are fairly earned by industrial organizers and others who manage our businesses and are necessary to enlist their services. Probably in most cases society does not overpay these leaders of industry. But some forms of profit, such as those derived solely from monopoly, especially from the monopoly of limited natural resources, are both too large and socially unearned. Clearly these should be controlled and absorbed by society.

DISTRIBUTION OF THE SOCIAL INCOME

One reason then why labor has not profited more by the great increase in wealth is that the other factors in production have laid claim to their shares also. There is good reason for believing, however, that the share of labor has been steadily growing greater all the time, and that today it gets a larger proportion of the social income than ever before. This fact is obscured by the great growth in population, which has more than doubled in the last hundred years in Europe and has shown a twentyfold increase in the United States. The larger income is divided among more people, and though each today gets more than his grandfather, there is not yet enough produced to make all rich. Indeed if the wealth of the United States were divided equally, it would not provide a competence for anybody. The difficulty is not merely that there is inequality in distribution, but that the need of a much greater production of wealth must also be met. Inequalities may be adjusted by such measures as progressive inheritance taxes, but resort to this or similar methods must not be so severe as to weaken the motives for the accumulation of capital. This must form one of the strongest reasons for rejecting the drastic proposals of socialism.

INCREASED COMMAND OVER COMFORTS

Improvements in production have, however, not merely increased the total output; they have greatly reduced the cost of many articles and have brought within the reach of the poorest consumers others which a century ago would have been unattainable. Improvements in transportation have served to bring an ever-increasing variety of products to market. The material progress of a people can be gaged fairly well by their consumption of certain semi-luxuries, such as tea, coffee, sugar, tobacco, beer, etc.; these show a steady increase during the past century.

Thus in the United States between 1871 and 1903 inclusive, the per capita consumption of coffee increased from 7.91 to 10.79 pounds, that of sugar from 36.2 pounds to 71.1 pounds, that of malt liquors from 6.1 gallons to 18.04 gallons, that of wheat and flour from 4.69 bushels to 5.81 bushels.[3]

A similar investigation for Great Britain shows an average increase of 40 per cent in a considerably larger list of the same character between 1860-64 and 1895-96. It must be admitted that there is much lack of economy in present consumption; there is often wasteful and positively injurious consumption, an illustration of which would be found by many persons in the increased consumption of malt liquors cited above. From a purely

[3] Adams and Sumner, *Labor Problems*, p. 523.

economic standpoint the enormous waste of war and the burdensome cost of military and naval armament must also be condemned.

THE FUTURE

The task of prophecy is usually a fruitless one, but at least it is now possible for us to indicate some of the lines along which reform is needed and the goal towards which the future of economic progress will probably move. The natural resources of the nation must be more carefully conserved and reckless destruction prevented; at the same time the monopolization of limited resources by private individuals or corporations must be rigidly restricted. The growth of trusts seems but the last step in a steady growth in size of the business unit and may be accepted as an economical method of industrial organization, but the evils of corporate financial management must be carefully guarded against.

The growth of labor organizations, on the other hand, must be admitted to be equally logical and desirable. While they often display monopolistic tendencies, yet our main reliance must be placed upon these agencies to secure bargains for laborers on terms of equality with their employers. But on behalf of wage-earners not easily organized we must resort to state intervention by means of factory and labor legislation in order to secure equitable labor contracts. Free competition which exposes women and children to the greed of unscrupulous employers is defended by no one today, and it is clearly recognized that legislation along these lines must be further extended, as for instance in the direction of industrial insurance, old-age pensions, adequate care for the unemployable, etc.

Improvements in our banking and currency system, an extension of banking facilities to the farming and artisan classes, the more careful regulation of railroad rates and reforms in methods of taxation—all are called for by the development and readjustment of industry. On the other hand, much remains to be done in the education of the mass of the people to habits of rational living and enjoyment. In the great cities housing conditions should be effectively regulated, sweat shops suppressed, intemperance discouraged, and where possible a love of art and outdoor life promoted. A more rational use of income would increase considerably the material well-being of the people.

Problems of distribution are still more insistent. No one who has the welfare of the laboring classes or of our democratic society at heart can view with approval the existence of widely separated classes, with disproportionate political and economic power. Greater equality in fortunes—a leveling up of incomes—must certainly be regarded as a sound social ideal. On the other hand, we have seen reason to reject the drastic remedies of socialism as a cure for the injustices of present methods of distribution or production. Improvement must come by conservative reform along the lines of our past development. In the last analysis all attempts to improve conditions permanently depend upon the character and capacity of the individual. Because of this fact education assumes great importance—education not merely in the art of production but also in that supreme art, the art of living.

TEST QUESTIONS

1. What improvement has been made since 1800 in the condition of the working class in the United States?

2. Along what lines has the progress in labor affairs taken place?

3. What progress has been made in the field of production? To what factors has this been due?

4. Has labor received its fair share of the benefits due to improved production?

5. Why has the institution of private property been continued in modern industrial society?

6. Why has society seen fit to place checks upon monopoly?

7. From the economic standpoint are military and war expenses justifiable?

8. What is the probable future tendency of development in corporate organizations? In labor organizations?

9. In the last analysis what factors determine true economic progress?

INDEX

Check Out More Titles From HardPress Classics Series In this collection we are offering thousands of classic and hard to find books. This series spans a vast array of subjects – so you are bound to find something of interest to enjoy reading and learning about.

Subjects:
Architecture
Art
Biography & Autobiography
Body, Mind &Spirit
Children & Young Adult
Dramas
Education
Fiction
History
Language Arts & Disciplines
Law
Literary Collections
Music
Poetry
Psychology
Science
…and many more.

Visit us at www.hardpress.net